Don Rumble is a man who carries the Holy Spirit's burden to see God's children made complete in Christ. He encourages the Church to be an expression of "Christ in you, the hope of glory" rather than settling for lesser goals. This book shares how God's call will one day transform the future of both the Church and the world. I encourage you to read its unique take on the Bible's revealed destiny for our planet.

—Bill Cadden
    Bible teacher, elder
    Saugerties Christian Fellowship, Saugerties, NY

I have known Don Rumble for many years and his writing has an overriding, dominant theme—the centrality of Christ. In a day in which man has too often claimed the glory that belongs only to God, Rumble encourages believers to give Christ His rightful place in our lives and in the Church. His title, *The Coming Increase of Christ in His House*, is quite fitting; the book addresses important prophetic themes and provides an encouraging view of the end times. You will be blessed as you read.

—Clay Sterrett
    Co-pastor
    Community Fellowship Church, Staunton, VA

I've known Don for close to 30 years. From where I stand, he has faithfully and humbly lived what he writes. His words are words of life because he has allowed the Holy Spirit to work them in and through his life. If our lives are Christlike we then become "lights of rev   l's purpose and plan for the Chu   is glory to us and through us. D   he "whole counsel of God". Wit   it-inspired insights in *The Comir   ouse*, Don has once again given us something truly Christ-centered. This

book is both a rich foundational teaching and a timely prophetic message for the Church.

    —Bill Furioso
        Bible teacher, missionary, author with At Christ's Table
        Ministries, elder
        Cornerstone Christian Fellowship, Rochester, NY

In *The Coming Increase of Christ in His House* Don Rumble gives prophetic insight into what is unfolding during our watch, our generation. The question is, *will we be aware of it*? Again, as always, Don points us to our relationship with Jesus. The challenge is not to be sidetracked but to press toward the fullness of God's purpose. May we continue to humble ourselves, yield to the Holy Spirit as He progressively unfolds His plan and awakens us all to His magnificent strategy for summing up all things in Christ Jesus.

    —Owen Carey
        Church planter, elder
        New Testament Christian Fellowship, Manchester, NH

Identifying the Fullness
of the Gentiles

the coming increase of

Christ

in His house

Identifying the Fullness
of the Gentiles

the coming increase of

Christ

in His house

DONALD RUMBLE

BRIDGE
LOGOS
FOUNDATION

Alachua, Florida 32615

Bridge-Logos
Alachua, FL 32615 USA

The Coming Increase of Christ in His House
Identifying the Fullness of the Gentiles
by Donald Rumble

Library of Congress Catalog Card Number: 2012940673

International Standard Book Number: 978-0-88270-810-2

TABLE OF CONTENTS

FOREWORD

ᓚᘏ

This well-written book deals with God's plans for the
Church, the Gentiles, and the Jews. With great insight, Don
lets us know what God's objectives are, and he gives intriguing
answers to these questions (among many others):

- What is the fullness of the Gentiles?

- How will this fullness affect the Church and Israel?

- What will God's house be like in the end times?

- What is the mystery of God's will?

- What is God's ultimate goal for humanity?

- How is God's righteousness defined?

- Is Church history about God's Kingdom or ours?

God is building a house for His people, a house that is
designed according to His eternal principles. In this book we
learn what our role is to be in the construction of God's house.
God's goal for each one of us is clear: to become like His Son,
who is perfect in every way. He wants us to bear His presence
wherever we are.

The Coming Increase of Christ in His House has clarified
so many things about the end times for me. It reminds me of
the importance of spending time with the Lord so that I will

learn to hear His voice. Don reveals God's mercy in a fresh and appealing way. He describes God's glory in a simple and direct way.

The book paints a vivid contrast between the house God is building and the Church as it exists today. He shows how churches have been contaminated by ungodly teachings and misunderstandings. He explains how Christ's presence will increase in our midst and this will cause the Jews to be jealous of what we will have.

It's very inspiring and exciting to contemplate these truths that are soundly based on God's Word. Even though most believers are oblivious to what God is doing behind the scenes, this book gives us a great deal to think about and look forward to—"life from the dead"—for both Jews and Gentiles.

I look forward to being at the feast God is preparing for His people. I look forward to the time when we will reign with Christ. I look forward to the time when the people of Israel will be saved.

This is one of the best books on eschatology that has ever been written. I know it will help God's people—both Jews and Gentiles—understand God's plans and purposes for the world He created. It will lead many people to repent and get involved in what He is doing today.

Thank you, Don, for giving us a book that clarifies many of the mysteries related to the end times. Your user friendly writing style opens new windows of understanding for each of us.

Lloyd B. Hildebrand
Publisher

PREFACE

The Scriptures reveal God's plan to build for His own eternal habitation a house according to His own specifications. Over the many centuries, He has been quietly proceeding with His agenda. At the same time, unbelievers live their lives oblivious both to what He is doing and of His ultimate goal for humanity.

Sadly, many Christians seem unaware as well. But God has called us to recognize and submit to Him in His purpose. This means not only yielding to His sovereign work in our lives by the Holy Spirit, but also when He speaks to us through others. Amazingly, God has chosen to demonstrate profound mercy by revealing himself both to and through imperfect people.

The revelation of God in Christ was perfect; the revelation of God in and through His people has great mixture. But God is at work in us to increase the purity and power of that expression and bring it to a measured fullness. When He does so, Israel will become jealous when she sees what God is doing, and then suddenly her eyes will be opened to the realization that God is revealing her long awaited Messiah through a people among the nations.

Throughout Church history, God's message has always been Christ; His strategy has been simple. He will bring the beauty and glory of His Son into increasing clarity in His Church before the eyes of the whole world. When this fullness of the Gentiles is realized, the nation of Israel will turn back to Him and God will bring the Earth into the final phase of His work among men.

INTRODUCTION

There is a Plan

God's plan for the Earth is unfolding before us. Though the nations are in turmoil, and spiritual darkness appears to hold them in its grip, the Lord continues to call people to himself. Many are hearing that summons and are stepping from darkness into the light.

But where are we headed? What specifically is the Lord's solution to the massive spiritual deception afflicting the Earth? And how are we to respond?

The Lord calls us to walk with Him in faith like Abraham did, and to believe that He will fulfill His promises. Central in our expectations is His guarantee to build His Church and to fill the Earth with His glory. Like Abraham, we are learning to differentiate between the initiatives of God and our attempts to do for Him what He promised to do. There is a vast difference between working with Him and simply doing whatever seems right in the light of certain Bible texts.

The question we face is whether we will recognize and yield to His timing and to His work among us. When others speak in His name, should we or should we not submit to what they are saying? The answer lies not in what position they hold but in whether they are revealing Christ, or their own thoughts, or even a desire to control others. Can we tell the difference? And just as importantly, how can we accurately reveal God to the world if we do not recognize His voice as we should in His own house?

Jesus knew His Father's voice intimately. And since His intent is to conform us into His likeness, in the coming years we will experience a greater clarity in hearing God's voice among His people. We will not achieve such a relationship through our own human efforts of spirituality, but only through His mercy. In fact, He is already drawing us to a greater intimacy with himself as He speaks to us through His Word this very day. What will be the result? He will confront the world with people who will bear His presence in every situation they face and who have no agenda except Christ Jesus and His glory.

Revealed Glory

God's strategy is to choose people from among the nations for His purpose. His choices do not reflect favoritism, but rather a plan to express His love for the whole Earth through His work in the lives of His people. How will He change us? He will mercifully reveal to us His glory. One cannot gain such an insight and then walk away unchanged.

Meanwhile, many among the nations, who do not know the Lord, proclaim themselves and their agendas for the Earth, not realizing it is the Lord who has given them a platform. And to the ultimate chagrin of many, He has done so for His fame, not theirs. It is His name that shall be made known throughout all the Earth.

Even among His own people, many have lost sight of the fact that it is the Lord's preeminence that we should be focused on, and it is only as we spend time beholding Him that we will have anything of eternal value to say. There simply is no other basis for accurately conveying Him to others.

Indeed, the Lord God of Heaven must come into greater clarity among His people before the eyes of the nations. Such beauty must then be seen as well by the nation of Israel as God's work comes to fullness among us. When His success in our midst stirs up jealousy in Israel, she will turn again to the God of her fathers. The grace of God that will be released among the nations at that time will then surpass what was granted two thousand years ago when Israel failed to receive her Messiah (Romans 11:12).

What will that increased expression of God's grace among the nations look like? It will reveal His escalating offensive against the influence of spiritual death oppressing the Earth. God has a solution to spiritual death; it is His life in us.

> To them God willed to make known what are the riches of the glory of this mystery among the Gentiles: which is Christ in you, the hope of glory. (Colossians 1:27)

His Church will then become increasingly known not for religious formalism, but for the experience and celebration of God's life manifest among us.

Ultimately, God will have a glorious house. His purpose, mercy, grace and commitment guarantee it; His Word decrees it. Its final appearance will be according to His specifications, not ours. In the days preceding His return He will sound forth from the midst of His Church His concluding words to the nations. His summation of what He has been saying for thousands of years will be explosive, concise, full of mercy and unapologetic.

Our cry to you Lord Jesus is that you will arise in our midst and build among us your glorious house. May your work in our lives reveal to the nations your glory rather than simply our interpretation of who you are.

PART ONE

Christ, God's Word to the Nations

"My name shall be great among the nations."

Malachi 1:11

CHAPTER 1

THE EMERGING CHILD OF PROMISE

God's Motive

Is it true that Christianity will experience an increased revelation of Christ in her midst and a massive growth in numbers? If so, how will we come to such glory? Is the answer to have more and larger mega churches? Should we try new evangelism programs? More focus on youth?

Before we address the above questions, let's examine this basic question. Why did the Lord arise in power among the nations to begin with? We know that He loved the world so much that He sent His Son to die and rise again for our salvation. No argument there. But there is another part to the answer. God turned to the nations to provoke the nation of Israel to jealousy, "I say then, have they stumbled that they should fall? Certainly not! But through their fall, to provoke them to jealousy, salvation has come to the Gentiles" (Romans 11:11). Any eschatology that claims insight into the early apostles' hearts, must address the issue of God's love and plans for Israel. The Lord intended to do something among the nations in order to get her attention.

But today, that nation does not appear to be very impressed with the Church's present relationship with God. Are we missing something? Should we try to look more Jewish, celebrating Old Testament holy days, keeping feasts, etc.? Did Paul teach such an approach?

Paul certainly loved Israel. He would have given up his own salvation if he thought that would save them (Romans 9:1-5). But we do not read of him teaching Gentile believers to keep feasts and Sabbaths to evangelize the Jews. Since the Colossian Church was made up primarily of Gentiles, wouldn't the apostle have encouraged them to observe Jewish holy days to impress Israel if that was God's strategy? Yet in his thought, Sabbath days, etc. are mere shadows and not the reality that cast them. "So let no one judge you in food or in drink, or regarding a festival or a new moon or sabbaths, which are a shadow of things to come, but the substance is of Christ" (Colossians 2:16,17).

A Love for Israel

While Paul loved Israel and longed to see her saved, he certainly held no illusions about some inherent goodness residing in his people. Today, some believers go perhaps a little far in identifying with the Jewish nation. To them, Christians must support Israel not only for her right to exist, but also in every action she takes. But Paul did not think this way. For example, he clearly opposed his nation's treatment of the churches. Even though he loved his people, he did not mince words when describing Israel as both spiritually fallen and under wrath, headed for destruction (1 Thessalonians 2:14-16). Today, some believers even go so far as to state that having a proper love for Israel is the foundation of the local church. But churches are to be built on Christ, not just His love for Israel.

Jesus had prophesied that great ruin would come to Israel within a generation:

20

Now as He drew near, He saw the city and wept over it, saying, "If you had known, even you, especially in this your day, the things that make for your peace! But now they are hidden from your eyes. For days will come upon you when your enemies will build an embankment around you, surround you and close you in on every side, and level you, and your children within you, to the ground; and they will not leave in you one stone upon another, because you did not know the time of your visitation. (Luke 19:41-44)

But when you see Jerusalem surrounded by armies, then know that its desolation is near. Then let those who are in Judea flee to the mountains, let those who are in the midst of her depart, and let not those who are in the country enter her. For these are the days of vengeance, that all things which are written may be fulfilled. But woe to those who are pregnant and to those who are nursing babies in those days! For there will be great distress in the land and wrath upon this people. And they will fall by the edge of the sword, and be led away captive into all nations. And Jerusalem will be trampled by Gentiles until the times of the Gentiles are fulfilled.

Assuredly, I say to you, this generation will by no means pass away till all things take place. (Luke 21:32)

In spite of this, Paul kept interceding on their behalf: "Brethren, my heart's desire and prayer to God for Israel is that they may be saved" (Romans 10:1). Would not God's mercy ultimately triumph for them? In response, the Lord began to show the apostle His redemptive plan and specifically how He would accomplish it. He would turn to the Gentiles and bring to fullness a work in their midst. This would so provoke the Jews that they would then turn back to Him.

> For I do not desire, brethren, that you should be ignorant of this mystery, lest you should be wise in your own opinion, that blindness in part has happened to Israel until the fullness of the Gentiles has come in. And so all Israel will be saved, as it is written: "The Deliverer will come out of Zion, And He will turn away ungodliness from Jacob. (Romans 11:25, 26)

So, what specifically is coming to fullness among the Gentiles? The New International Version phrases Paul's comment such that when the full *number* of Gentiles comes in, all Israel will be saved. But the word "number" is not in the Greek manuscripts. Paul simply informs us that some sort of "fullness" is coming among us.

Worship, Wait, and Obey

To answer our question, let's consider Paul's teaching concerning Israel's basic failure. They were zealous for God, but they were ignorant of His righteousness and sought to establish their own. Then when their Messiah stood in their midst, they failed to submit to the righteousness of God.

> For they being ignorant of God's righteousness, and seeking to establish their own righteousness, have not submitted to the righteousness of God. (Romans 10:3)

So how should we define God's righteousness? Clearly, it is not something we can apprehend by keeping laws and rules. Long before the Old Testament laws were given, the Lord declared Abraham to be righteous simply because he believed and obeyed Him.

God promised Abraham that he would become the father of a multitude, that through him all nations would be blessed—indeed, he would be heir of the world (Genesis 17:4; 22:17, 18; Romans 4:13). This promise would not be realized by human efforts but by simply believing the One who had made the promise. The problem was that to become father to a multitude, Abraham would have to father at least one child. However, as much as he and Sarah tried to conceive, they simply could not. When Sarah suggested that her husband become involved with Hagar, the servant girl, it seemed like an acceptable solution. But it wasn't.

There is no record that the Lord spoke to Abraham for 13 years after his initial involvement with Hagar and the birth of their son Ishmael. Imagine thinking for years that your child is the guarantee of God's promised multiplication only to one day hear Him say otherwise. Yet, God did not return to condemn Abraham; He came in mercy to reveal and interrupt Abraham's misguided zeal. Today we need God in His mercy to interrupt His Church.

Those who bring forth spiritual Ishmaels[1] today are not false prophets any more than Abraham was. Today, many of God's people are His friends; we love Him, hear His voice, and in some measure, see His purpose. The problem is, like Abraham, we simply don't wait for the Lord to bring to pass what He has promised.

The Christian life is not about doing works for God, or trying to help Him fulfill His promises. Rather, we are to worship, wait, and obey. In Scripture, to wait is to expect. It is not the waiting of one in a recliner chair as he naps. Rather, it is the expectation of one at the starting line of a footrace as he anticipates the sound of the starter pistol. Believers expect the Lord to move actively in their lives. As we see what He is doing, we can then cooperate with Him in His work. Jesus lived such a life perfectly.

God promised Abraham that he would have many descendants; the fulfillment of this promise meant multiplication. Today we who are of faith are Abraham's children (Galatians

---

1   A spiritual Ishmael is simply whatever God's people attempt to bring forth in His name instead of waiting for His grace to lead us forward in His own timing.

3:7). As believers, we inherently know that we are to multiply. Massive numbers of people will yet come into God's Kingdom. But His promise is not based on the Church's attempts to multiply, but on His own faithfulness.

Abraham's Faith

Genuine faith is more than mere mental agreement with sound Christian teaching. It has to do with lifestyle. Abraham left his city and pursued the Lord and His purpose. He left what was comfortable and went out, not knowing where he was going (Hebrews 11:8).

When he got to the Land of Promise, he lived there as though it was a foreign land, even though God had promised it to him. He did not start announcing to all who could hear that it now belonged to him. Nor did he start killing Canaanites to take it over. Many years later Joshua would express faith by killing Canaanites, but Abraham expressed his faith by living peaceably with them. Timing is crucial; God reveals His Kingdom when we move in harmony with Him according to His schedule.

Treating the land as foreign and not as his own possession, Abraham lived in tents, temporary dwellings with no foundations. Permanence would only come when God began building. So he waited for the city with foundations designed and built by God (Hebrews 11:9, 10). All the Old Testament children of Abraham who lived by faith looked forward to something more than mere real estate in the Middle East. They saw themselves as pilgrims seeking a homeland. Therefore, God prepared a city for them (Hebrews 11:12-16).

But how would He begin construction? Obviously, He would have to lay the foundation. Looking forward, Isaiah prophesied that the foundation would be a precious and tested cornerstone (Isaiah 28:16). Many years earlier, Abraham had also looked ahead and recognized God himself walking into the land and becoming the basis for the heavenly project (John 8:56).

The Bible concludes with a vision of that city. It is actually the Lamb's bride, and her origin is Heaven (Revelation 21:9, 10). So among other things, God's work is a house, a city, and a bride.

In many ways, we who are Abraham's children are still waiting. Since Jesus said that He would do the building, we recognize the Church age as the time of construction (Matthew 16:18). We must cooperate with Him as He builds His house, His city. We do not have the right to organize corporate ministries to extend God's Kingdom. We only have the right to worship, wait, and obey. We are involved with His project; it is not our own. True faith believes in the One who said He would build His Church. We will seek to only move in oneness with Him. Human initiative to "get the job done" will continue to bring forth spiritual Ishmaels in our day. But the child of promise is also emerging from the heavenly initiative. Can we tell the difference? Is it not important to ask the Lord to help us in this matter?

CHAPTER 2

SUBMISSION TO GOD'S RIGHTEOUSNESS

God's Priorities

Two thousand years ago when God revealed His righteousness in Christ, Israel failed to recognize the time of their visitation. As a nation, they did not submit to Him and they sought to establish their own righteousness. Today, the Church faces the same option. Will we yield to the Lord, His work and His timing, or will we launch on His behalf works revealing our strength and ingenuity? This begs some questions: Is Church history about God's Kingdom or ours? Will it be His glory or ours revealed among us?

Frankly, we need to answer these questions correctly. History is not about man; it is about God and His work among us. At the end of history, we will not be marveling at the great accomplishments of educated people; we will be in wonder at God's glorious grace that enabled His people to do great things. When we view His finished work among us, it will be His glory beautifying us. History is His story.

Even today, we must recognize His priorities if we would have accurate spiritual insight. We must be impressed with what impresses Him and we must detest what He hates. When rich men brought bags of money into the temple, many were impressed while Jesus yawned. Then when the widow brought in her small gift, Jesus cheered while most missed the point. In other words, it is possible to experience the Lord in a particular event and wrongly interpret His priorities. What a tragedy to encounter Him and to not know Him. So what is the solution? We must humble ourselves to learn His ways.

The Fruit of Righteousness

Israel had experienced much history with the Lord, but many had failed to learn His ways. As a result, when God's righteousness was revealed in Christ, they did not submit (Romans 10:3). The miracle of the incarnation is that God himself walked among His people; the great tragedy was that most of them did not receive Him. But to as many as did so, to them He gave the right to become His children. Submission to God's righteousness had to do with properly receiving Him as He was revealed among them. Today, such surrender remains the key to a spiritually fruitful life.

Paul informs us that Christ himself is God's righteousness (1 Corinthians 1:30). We experience Him as such when we repent of our sins and receive Him and His rule in our lives. On this, evangelical Christians agree. God then receives us as His own people because He has cleansed us by His blood and filled us with His own holy presence. How awesome is this precious gift of righteousness that was purchased for us at so great a cost to Him.

But righteousness is more than a gift given; it is a fruit grown (Hebrews 12:11). God not only gives spiritual birth to a people, He then works to conform us to His likeness. The fruit of His work in us is to be an increase of His love, kindness, goodness, and so forth (Galatians 5:22, 23). He has purposed that the fruit of righteousness would develop in the Church.

Such is the Holy Spirit's ministry. He is working to bring forth in us a visible increased expression of Christ. Such growth will only come as we embrace the Cross, as we turn from our desires and welcome His. When we do so, others will see in us a little less of the nature of man and a little more of the nature of God. He does this work in us so that He can entrust influence to us in the lives of others.

Spiritual Influence

But who should influence the Church the most? Should it be those who are the most powerful speakers? Or should it be those who consistently embrace the Cross? Highly influential leaders who have not first submitted to Calvary as a lifestyle have done much damage in God's house.

We simply *do not need* more "ministries" holding forth good ideas on what we should do next. What we *do need* is less of man and more of Christ. May He increase in His house and help us all to decrease in the process.

Yet with all the spiritual mixture evident in God's house, we are still confronted by His righteousness in the lives of believers around us. How are we to submit? The question is simple when the Scriptures clearly articulate His will in a particular situation. We will yield to His Word.

Perhaps He might even make His desires known to us through a dream or a vision. Often though, other believers will claim to speak to us on behalf of the Lord. At this point do we submit or not?

If one claims to speak for God but only reveals his own heart, he brings an element of spiritual control. Too often, people claiming to speak for the Lord have both misrepresented Him and brought damage to others.

Because mistakes have been many, the temptation is to

try to escape the learning process. But we cannot. God will still address us through those around us. Recognizing and submitting to Him is crucial if we want to keep from making the same mistake as Israel.

When Paul preached to the Thessalonians, they recognized that something greater was occurring than merely a man speaking his own mind. In receiving him and what he said, they received the Lord.

> For this reason we also thank God without ceasing, because when you received the word of God which you heard from us, you welcomed it not as the word of men, but as it is in truth, the word of God, which also effectively works in you who believe. (1 Thessalonians 2:13)

But not all speak with the same spiritual clarity as Paul. How do we keep from coming under the control of others in the Church? One of the main differences between true Christianity and certain cults is our freedom to make practical personal decisions with a clear conscience. As adults we have many daily choices to make. Sometimes those around us will disagree with our course.

Accountability

So the question remains. Should we be accountable to others in the local church? Some who have answered in the affirmative have not been totally pure in their motives. In order to bring others into submission to themselves, they have strongly promoted the accountability of believers to appointed leaders. Often, such an approach has resulted in a legalistic definition of church order, the imposition of men's ideas, and the commensurate loss of believers' freedom to personally hear from God.

So how should this work? In normal Christian relationships, accountability is not imposed; it is freely offered. When we truly love others, we offer them our hearts. We open up and become vulnerable to their thoughts and ideas. Because they are important to us, what they think about certain decisions we are making becomes important to us as well. In seeking their counsel, we become accountable.

How about Christian leaders? Are they left out of the equation? They are if they expect people to submit to them based simply on their holding a position in the Church. In that case, they are misrepresenting spiritual authority, which is not positional like secular authority. I do not have authority over another in God's house because I hold a position of leadership. But if by the grace of God He sends me to speak to someone, I go with the authority to represent Him. Inherent in the word I bring, will be the enabling grace for the hearer to do what He is saying. That is why the gospel is not just *about* God's power; it *is* His power (Romans 1:16).

How we need a restoration of true spiritual authority in God's house. Not only must believers submit to the grace of God in those who lead, but godly leaders must also love His people and be as vulnerable to God's grace in them. No one is exempt from submitting to the righteousness of God.

Spiritual authority is not about getting people to respond to us; it is about helping them to respond to Christ. As we are filled with His presence, and function according to His grace, those around us will have the opportunity to submit to Christ, the righteousness of God.

Israel failed two thousand years ago to submit to His righteousness and they missed their Messiah. We also will miss Him in our generation if we fail to recognize Him in the lives of those to whom He has connected us.

CHAPTER 3

AN APOSTOLIC PEOPLE

God's Spokesman

It is a tragedy that those who do not presently know Christ stand condemned before Him without even knowing they are spiritually lost. And the Christian Church stands right in their midst with the presence of God in our hearts. What should we do? What should be our priority? First of all, our call is to love the Lord with all of our hearts and to submit to Him as He reveals himself by His Spirit, through His Word, and through other people in our lives.

Sometimes I think God's program for the nations would be further along if He spoke only through divine encounters, or through angels. But amazingly, God has chosen to also reveal himself through imperfect people.

Perhaps it would be easier for us in the Church to submit to His Word if the believers around us were just a little more humble, kind, gentle, etc. But sometimes He chooses to speak to us through one of the more obviously (to us, anyway) flawed brethren. How well do we respond at such times?

And here is the question we must face if we desire to impact the world around us. How can we expect unbelievers to gladly receive the Lord's Word through us if we ourselves do not receive His spokesmen to us? We must face this question squarely. For too long the Church has believed that all we need for successful ministry is the truth that can save men's souls. But God has determined to reveal more through us about himself than mere factual information. He wants to confront the Earth with His righteousness. And His righteousness is a Person, even Christ himself (1 Corinthians 1:30).

Granted, we often appear just as flawed in the eyes of the lost as do those in the Church who address us, but the difference is this: we already know the Lord and His Word. We should recognize when He is speaking to us through someone. When such an event occurs, we must submit to the righteousness of God. We must bend our knee to His lordship. His will and not ours must carry the day in our decisions. Then when He sends us to others, whether they are believers or not, we will not promote mere facts; we will reveal the truth, the person of Christ. He is our message, our agenda.

An Apostolic People

The New Testament has much to say about apostolic ministry. The word "apostle" means one sent on a mission. For the Church to again be an apostolic people, we must recover the truth that God himself is actively building His own house. He has not called us to work separately from Him; He was quite clear—Jesus would build His Church (Matthew 16:18). Whatever ministry we have among His people, it is only valid to the degree that it is in submission to His initiative and in cooperation with His enabling grace. It is only in this context that the idea of spiritual authority makes any sense.

The word "authority" has to do with the right to speak or to act. Who has the right to speak or act in any given circumstance?

Very simply, it is those whom God has sent. An apostolic people will spend time with the Lord, they will learn His voice and His heart. They will sense His orchestration in the various daily/weekly events of their lives. Faith will arise in their hearts to act and speak accordingly as they recognize God's sovereignty in sending them into various circumstances

But there is a problem. Some Christians seem to align themselves more with Deism than with biblical Christianity. This philosophy teaches that God is not actively involved with His creation. Rather, He has set it up to run pretty much without His help according to scientific principles. Obviously, this is not good theology in any application, but when it is applied to God's house, it is quite destructive. The idea is that after God started the Church, He basically set it up to run according to good organizational principles. As long as people know their places within the organization and do their jobs without rocking the boat, the local church will do just fine.

The result of such an approach is what we see in much of the Church in Western civilization—a Christianity that is no longer apostolic. No wonder our culture is so aberrant; it reflects the spiritual dysfunction in the Church, the one entity designed to illuminate the nations. The root of the problem is that the Church has lost her spiritual authority; she doesn't understand her destiny, and she cannot find her prophetic voice.

The True Nature of the War

If God has called us to submit to His righteousness, revealed by His Spirit both in His Word and in those He sends to us, how do we recognize it? For starters, one clear mark of God's righteousness is that it conveys truth without anyone necessarily saying anything. Paul informs us that it confronts those who insist that someone needs to either go to Heaven to see if Christ really *is* there or else go down to the pit to prove that He really is *not* there.

But the righteousness of faith speaks in this way, "Do not say in your heart, 'Who will ascend into heaven?' " (that is, to bring Christ down from above) or, "'Who will descend into the abyss?' " (that is, to bring Christ up from the dead). (Romans 10:6, 7)

In other words, the active increase of the nature of God in His people (i.e., His own righteousness) communicates the reality of the resurrected Christ to those who do not know Him. God has an answer for those who think that before they can yield to Christ, He must personally appear to them. In a word, God has placed before them a people in whom the fruit of His righteousness is growing and increasing.

The growing fruit of righteousness, the increasing expression of God's nature in those who seek His face and embrace the Cross, will shine like a light confronting the darkened souls of humanity. Let us be clear, the growing confrontation between light and darkness in our nation will be not only between those who preach the gospel and unbelievers. It will also be between those who yield to the righteousness of God and those who do not, whether they be believers or not. The sad fact is that many believers hate the Cross—not as a religious symbol, but as a lifestyle.

For even when Christ came to the Earth two thousand years ago, many spoke from the Scriptures, and many did not. But the confrontation between light and darkness was not primarily around the various rabbinical debates concerning the Law and the prophets, but about the revelation of the person of Christ. He was the Father put into human terms, the Light to illuminate the world. Men either hated that Light or ran to it. It is no different today.

We must love and embrace the Lord when He reveals His beauty and our failures; we must run to Him even when His Word confronts our self-love, pride, and lust, etc. The true nature of spiritual warfare is not primarily about saying prayers against Satan while experiencing high-powered worship. It is about submitting to God's righteousness. If we do not recognize Him, we will fail to respond to Him appropriately, and like Israel, we will simply go off establishing our own righteousness (Romans 10:3).

For example, many of God's people today stand confidently before Him because of their seeming success at preaching, their ability to lead a worship service, and prophetic ministry, etc. Yet, if God were to send to them someone with a word of even the slightest adjustment, they would react and reject it. Why? To them, the spoken word undermines their determined basis for standing before the Lord. "God has accepted me. He approves of my lifestyle. Look at how He blesses when I preach, counsel, etc." Since Christ is God's righteousness, and they do not want to hear His Word through someone who challenges their confidence, they have established their own basis of acceptance before God.

At this point, they stand upon a flawed foundation. When the inevitable shakings come, they will be vulnerable to satanic suggestions to doubt God's Word, be divisive toward others, and harbor an unforgiving attitude, etc.

Also at this point, the question becomes just how effective such a one really is in the area of spiritual warfare. Successful kingdom living is about more than having what appears to be an anointed ministry in the Church; it is about standing firmly on Christ the foundation no matter what winds and waves of life we encounter.

Today God is building a house designed according to His own "specs," according to His own eternal priorities. He intends for it to stand forever and to express what was in His heart before the foundation of the world. Since we do not know what the final product will look like, we must submit to His eternal perspective; His view is better than ours.

CHAPTER 4

SAVING THE CHURCH

God's Standard

God has determined to fashion His people according to His own design. His standard is nothing less than the likeness of His own Son; He intends to conform us to the image of Christ, "For whom He foreknew, He also predestined to be conformed to the image of His Son, that He might be the firstborn among many brethren" (Romans 8:29). How foolish to think that we could ever form ourselves according to His eternal objective.

But surely there is something we can do. We can respond with faith both in Christ's holy character and in His power to fulfill in us what He has started. In fact, if we will believe in our hearts that God has raised Him from the dead and verbally confess Him, God will save us. To be saved (Greek, SOZO) is to be made whole, to be delivered. Not only do the lost need to be saved, the Church desperately needs to as well.

We tend to think of salvation only in terms of being saved from eternal damnation. Once we are born again, we are saved. But Scripture also refers to salvation in ways other than our initial rebirth experience. Jesus would heal people and then tell them that their faith had saved them, i.e., made them physically sound. Paul spoke to those already born of the Spirit in the Roman Church concerning how they could be saved (Romans 10:6-10). James also informed believers that if they received God's Word, it would save their souls (James 1:21).

To be made whole spiritually is to become like Christ, God's standard for us. We fall so far short of Christ's image that many have accepted substandard living as normal. But what is usual is not necessarily appropriate. The truth is that the only normal man who ever walked the Earth was Jesus; it took God to be a man.

The Journey Into Wholeness

So how will we ever become normal? Paul says we must confess the Lord Jesus. We do not speak His name as some sort of technique to achieve psychological wholeness. We speak of Him because we love Him. We confess Him when we pray, worship, exhort other believers, teach the Word, and evangelize, etc. The act of declaring Him expresses the faith in our hearts that He is alive and well, ruling the nations. For the rest of our lives we will speak of the Lord Jesus, believing that God has raised Him from the dead. As we do so, God will conform us to the likeness of His Son.

Clearly, the journey into wholeness is not a weekend trek. It will not suffice to simply attend a conference dedicated to making people spiritually sound. Even if we graduate from an accredited Bible school with a degree in spiritual or psychological counseling, we are not any more normal than the ones to whom we speak. In fact, the more knowledge we have, the prouder we tend to be.

God holds before us an unattainable goal; we are to become like His Son, who was perfect. The fact that flawed people speak of perfection as normal may seem humorous at first. But it is only funny (actually it is really quite sad) when we present ourselves as something other than the imperfect people we really are. We are all on a journey into wholeness; there is no room for pride.

Lord, deliver your Church from experts. An expert is one who has arrived somewhere and has the answers for the rest of us. But the Lord calls us all to be His disciples; a disciple is a learner. And we are all in this together, learning Christ and His ways.

So how far along this road will we actually go in our lifetimes? Certainly, we will not achieve perfection this side of eternity. Outsiders sometimes like to point their fingers at the Church and celebrate the obvious flaws in our midst. "Why don't you guys just quit and settle for the reality of the human condition? Stop preaching righteousness. All you're doing is making us feel guilty. And besides, we see plenty of failures in your own midst."

But God has made a promise. If we continue to trust Him, He will vindicate us. For, "Whoever believes on Him will not be put to shame" (Romans 10:11). There is an end in sight. God is bringing His purpose among us to fullness among the nations. Herein lies Israel's hope.

Apostolic Fruit

God's goal is nothing less than the revelation of His Son among the nations. Basically, His message can be summed up in one word: Christ. When He called Paul to be an apostle, He did not give him a five-year plan for reaching the nations, He simply revealed His Son. The gospel Paul preached was not according to man, i.e., in harmony with human nature; it was according to God. What he preached did not come from man, for a message from a flawed source would only produce a flawed result.

Instead, Paul sat in the presence of Perfection and described to others the beauty of what he saw. He was not called to simply talk *about* Christ; he was called to preach Christ, i.e., to actually impart through word and deed the presence and power of the One he was presenting (Galatians 1:16). In other words, preaching the gospel is more than a transfer of information; it is the impartation of a Person. In a word, such an event is miraculous. To put it another way, the gospel is not *about* the power of God; it *is* the power of God.

Quite simply, God has called us to bear His presence into the various circumstances of our lives. His Kingdom really is that uncomplicated. Our great need is not for more theological degrees; it is for more of Him to be revealed both in us and through us. Our great need is for Christ. The world does not need the Church to be more visible; the world needs the Lord to be seen more clearly in His people. May there be less of self and more of Him, less human strength and agendas; and more of the power of Heaven manifested through weak human vessels filled with faith in the abiding power of God.

In light of the great spiritual darkness of our day, many try to stir the Church to action by challenging us to go to the lost. But ministry is not about going, it is about being sent. *["And how shall they preach unless they are sent?"]*—Greek, APOSTELLO (Romans 10:15). The word apostle means one who has been sent on a mission. Jesus did not simply come to the Earth; He was sent. He is the Apostle of our faith. His primary mission was to reveal the One who sent Him. Our mission is to be the same. We are called to be an apostolic people. As we come to intimately know the Lord, we are then to respond to Him as He sends us to others.

Many today speak of the restoration of apostles to the Church. And we hear of some who claim to be apostles. But the claim to be one and the ability to teach on the subject doesn't necessarily prove their validity. We must judge ministry by the fruit. What is being produced? Effective apostolic ministry is validated when the people themselves become apostolic. In other words, they increasingly represent God and His interests in their circumstances.

When apostles preach some other agenda than the person of Christ, those to whom they minister will also promote something other than Christ. Usually, they become proponents of their particular movement or the leader(s) thereof. Too many today promote streams, movements, methods of church building, etc. Such an approach will not bring abiding change to the Earth. But God's plan is well underway. God will give true apostles to His Church again. And in every place He sends them, people in love with Christ and bearing His presence and interest will emerge among the nations.

CHAPTER 5

MAKING HIM KNOWN

The Road to God

God revealed himself in Jesus Christ two thousand years ago in the nation of Israel. While most of the world missed both the event and its significance, there were those who received Him, gained understanding and led many to righteousness. At the end of history when Christ returns, no one will miss either the event or its importance. All will come face to face with Him and have to give account of their lives.

Prior to that day, God will bring to fullness all that He has purposed to do on Earth through the ministry of the Holy Spirit. The question we face today is whether we believe the Spirit of God will succeed in all He has been sent to accomplish. Will the Holy Spirit be as victorious in Church history as Christ was two thousand years ago?

Just as Jesus was sent to reveal the Father, so also the Spirit has come to reveal the Son:

> And I will pray the Father, and He will give you another
> Helper, that He may abide with you forever—the Spirit

of truth, whom the world cannot receive, because it neither sees Him nor knows Him; but you know Him, for He dwells with you and will be in you. I will not leave you orphans; I will come to you. (John 14:16 -18)

However, when He, the Spirit of truth, has come, He will guide you into all truth; for He will not speak on His own authority, but whatever He hears He will speak; and He will tell you things to come. He will glorify Me, for He will take of what is Mine and declare it to you. (John 16:13-14)

If we are responding to the Spirit, we are both learning and revealing Christ. Two thousand years ago, Jesus' own disciples failed at first to grasp that the God who fills eternity was revealing himself among them. Time after time, in one circumstance after another, Jesus would accurately discover and make known the Father's heart and purpose to those around Him. In other words, His life as a man revealed to those He loved the road of access to the Father.

As Jesus began to prepare the disciples for His departure, He expected them to already know the road He would take. "And where I go you know, and the way {Greek, HODOS—a road} you know" (John 14:4).

He was going to the Father. He had been doing so in front of them for many months. Surely now they had a clear understanding of God's road. But their words revealed that they did not. "Lord, we do not know where you are going, and how can we know the way?" (John 14:5).

His response startled them and amazes us. Jesus himself is the road of access (John 14:6). And His instruction was that apart from Him no one could *come* (notice that He did not say *go*) to the Father. The locale of God for relationship could now only be found in the Son. Jesus' heart was filled with the presence of the One who had sent Him. To put it another way,

Jesus had come relationally to the place where He was about to go physically.

From now on, anyone's sincere search for God would bring the seeker directly to Christ. Jesus had become both the road to the goal and the goal at the end of the road. God had established such a union of intimacy and expression with His Son that whoever looked upon Jesus saw the Father (John 14:9).[2]

The fact that He came as a man to such an experience of oneness with His Father while still on the Earth, testifies to us of God's strategy for His redeemed people.

The Spirit's Mission

The Holy Spirit has been sent to the Earth to bring forth on Earth the locale where God can be found relationally. As God was in Christ two thousand years ago, so now the presence of God is to be found in the Church. Too often though, what is found in His house is an external form of religion more than the vitality of a living and increasing intimacy with Him.

So the questions arise again: Will the Holy Spirit be as successful in Church history as Jesus was two thousand years ago? Will He succeed in revealing Christ in and through the Church? Will the nations be able to look and behold the consistent expression of the glory of God in His people? Or will we continue to draw attention to ourselves, to our leaders, to our methods, and to our successes in His name? To put the question another way: "Is there a way forward from where we are that will bring us to God's destination for us?"

Very simply, we must gather to Him. Jesus taught that in His Father's house there were many dwelling places (John 14:2). His strategy for establishing God's purpose on Earth was to ascend back to the Father and then from Heaven to prepare a place for

---

2   This is not to suggest that Jesus somehow attained to the status of deity; He was as much God at His birth as He was throughout His life. God had become a human, and as the God-man, He lived out for us in human terms the perfect expression of both humanity and deity. As a man, He grew in wisdom, stature, and in favor with His Father and with those to whom He had been sent. (Luke 2:52)

each of us in God's house. If Christ has established a unique place for each of us in His house, then one of our top priorities must be to find where we belong. But how do we do so?

In His dialogue, the Lord made it clear that He would send the Spirit of truth to abide in us. He would not leave us as orphans; He would indeed come to us. In fact, as He prepared a place for each of us, He would come and receive us to himself so that where He is, we could be also. The key to finding our place in God's house is to pursue Him; the whole point is that He would draw us to himself.

God is not drawing us primarily into a ministry; He is drawing us to himself. But in finding Him, we then discover His heart for those to whom He sends us. Remember, God has not sent His Spirit to reveal mighty men and women of God, and their ministry to others. He has come to reveal Christ. It is as we discover Him in the situations of life that we then have something of eternal value to say to others.

If You Ask Anything in My Name

So also, Jesus came to Earth not primarily to minister among men according to their needs, but to reveal the One who had sent Him. This mission also included dying on the Cross. The revelation of God, not the need of man, was His primary motivation.

But as He sought to know and to reveal the One who had sent Him, Jesus found himself on the road to the Cross. The Cross was the inevitable consequence of knowing and making known His Father. God's amazing love for the world along with His simultaneous hatred for our sin seemed like irreconcilable aspects of His heart. But these two opposite extremes met and were fulfilled in the person of Christ when He who knew no sin became sin and then died, breaking its power.

Christ's death and resurrection two thousand years ago just outside Jerusalem were the greatest price ever paid and the greatest victory ever won in human history. Mercy and truth kissed and divine love and justice were revealed. The revelation of God was and is the whole point of human history.

In fact, Jesus seemed almost overly zealous that His disciples get the point. If you have seen Me, you have seen the Father. You must believe that the Father is in Me and that I am in Him. The words that I speak are really His words. The works are His works. If you have a hard time believing what I'm saying, believe on account of the works that I'm doing. You must believe in Me. (See John 14:9 -12).

What was Jesus saying? Very simply, the Father had come and received the Son to himself so that where the Father was, there the Son was also. Jesus lived His whole life abiding in the One who had sent Him. Whether He was in the midst of Pharisees, the tax collectors, etc, the Father was there also. Wherever the Son went, He made His Father known.

Jesus wanted the disciples to accept and believe that He had in fact succeeded in consistently knowing and revealing the Father's heart no matter what the circumstance. His works proved His point. In the light of this truth and in this particular context, Jesus then made one of the most startling promises in all of the New Testament. Amazing things would happen if we understood what He was saying and believed Him.

> Most assuredly, I say to you, he who believes in Me, the works that I do he will do also; and greater works than these he will do, because I go to My Father. And whatever you ask in My name, that I will do, that the Father may be glorified in the Son. If you ask anything in My name, I will do it. (John 14:12-14)

Jesus did not say that He would give us whatever we wanted. The Christian life is not about us getting what we desire. The Holy Spirit has been sent to reveal Christ. If we will draw near to Him and find His heart in the situations of life, He will do through us works impossible for us to do in our own strength—works that will glorify the Lord Jesus.

CHAPTER 6

GOD'S STRATEGY

Choices

God has a strategy for filling the Earth with His glory. To understand His approach, it is essential that we spend time with Him and discover in His Word the way forward from where we are. While many have seemingly good ideas concerning the road to take, the truth is that we need to hear clearly from Him.

One obvious ingredient in the Lord's eternal plan is that He chooses people. While it is true that He shows no partiality or favoritism (Acts 10:34), it is also true that He makes strategic choices among us for tasks to be done in His name. Such is His prerogative and His right.

When God determined that Esau would serve Jacob, He was not predetermining who would ultimately go to Heaven and who would not. Rather, His focus was on a task to be accomplished, a job to be done on Earth. The older would serve the younger. Clearly, Esau's service would not take place in the afterlife from hell, but on Earth while they both lived.

Loving Some; Hating Others

Nothing would deter the Lord from His plan and priorities. The Scripture says that He loved Jacob and hated Esau. What does this statement mean? Jesus used the same word *hate* when describing how His disciples were to love Him more than their own families (Luke 14:26, Matthew 10:37). As much as those closest to us may try to deter us from following Him, Christ must be our first choice. We must choose Him above all that is dear to us. At the same time, the New Testament clearly directs us not to hate our families but to love them (1Timothy 5:8).

So how does this work? In some parts of the world today when a young man decides to follow the Lord, his relatives may try everything they know to change his mind. Those observing may even speak about how this son hates his family. "Look how he disregards the counsel of his parents." But the son, though misunderstood by all, has eternal life and now carries the hope for his family's eternal destiny. Even if his loved ones are so offended that they kill him, the way he dies will carry the seeds of Holy Spirit conviction to hopefully turn their hearts toward Him.

So also, God loves the whole world, even though there are many like Esau in it (John 3:16). We must never doubt this truth. Yet nothing will dissuade Him from His chosen strategy for filling the Earth with His glory. He will continue to choose and to call men and women to himself for the sake of those around them.

Today God continues to make choices among people that through His chosen vessels He might make known His love for all. While it might seem that God loves some and hates others, such "hatred" is not an emotional revulsion coupled with rejection. Rather, it is a reflection of His priority to make known in His own way and in His own time His love for the nations.

What am I saying? Jesus prayed not for the world but for those who would believe on Him, "I pray for them. I do not pray for the world but for those whom You have given Me, for they are Yours" (John 17:9). Was He rejecting the world? No, He came that the world through Him might be saved. Rather, He was focused on Heaven's strategy. God had chosen some men out from the world. Then as these disciples became one, the world would be able to believe.

God also made a choice among nations. Even though He so loved the world and sent His Son to die for humanity's sins, He did not send Him to every country but to Israel. Then because Jesus was faithful there in His sphere of service, the ultimate result would be that many among the nations would glorify God for His mercy (Romans 15:8, 9).

In Romans 9, Paul is not teaching God's predetermined eternal rejection of Esau. Rather, He is teaching God's eternal calling of Jacob. Through the younger brother He intended to establish His purpose among men. Though He loved Esau, His strategy of choosing Jacob would be seen as hatred toward the older twin. Nevertheless, no matter what men said or thought, He would never be deterred from His plan of bringing forth the Savior of the world through the line of Jacob. As a result of His dealings with Jacob, Esau could then experience God in a new way.

Think about the tension between the two brothers. When Jacob deceived his father and stole the patriarchal blessing due his brother, he had to flee for his life because Esau wanted to kill him. But some years later, God required Jacob to go back and face the music. Then when he heard that Esau was coming to meet him with 400 men, he began to fear for his life (Genesis 32, 33).

But no matter what Jacob tried, sending presents, referring to himself as Esau's servant, and so forth, his brother kept coming. Finally, Jacob was left alone and he wrestled with God.

After struggling all night, he cried out for the Lord to bless him. It was at this point that God changed Jacob's name to Israel and bestowed the blessing. But what blessing did the Lord grant? The answer seems to be that God arose and moved upon Esau's heart and changed something deep inside of him. Then when Esau saw his younger brother, he ran, fell on his neck, kissed him, and they wept. The feelings of rejection and the desire for murder had been removed.

Present Implications

Someone recently suggested that the name for the Jewish nation in today's Middle East should be Jacob instead of Israel. While being facetious, his point is well taken. Today Jacob exists as a nation because God has called him back to the land of promise. There the Lord and His estranged servant are headed toward a great confrontation, a wrestling match, if you will. Meanwhile, the nation is full of self-strength and is surrounded by the descendants of Esau. Even though many politicians and national leaders have tried to bring peace to the Middle East, none have succeeded. But there is coming a day when Jacob will again find himself standing alone, having run out of ideas on how to survive.

It is at such times of danger and seeming isolation that people often cry out to God for help. It will be no different this time. The Lord will hear Jacob's cry, change his heart and bring him into relationship with himself through Israel's destined Messiah Jesus. One part of the great heavenly blessing to come upon Israel will be that the Lord will arise to bring an amazing change of heart upon Esau. Deep repentance and reconciliation will occur between these descendants of Abraham and the world will marvel. Breathtaking change is yet to come upon the Muslim nations of the Middle East because of God's great love and dealings with Israel (Isaiah 19).

To be clear, the Lord makes choices among the inhabitants of the Earth but not because some are more deserving than others. There simply is no room for pride or elitism. Our God loves the whole world. And He intends to fill the planet with His glory before this age ends. But He will not be talked out of His strategy.

Let us draw near to Him and discover His heart for the ones He sends us to. The consequences of our obedience to Him will amaze us and change the Earth. While millions might seem to be hated and rejected by the Lord, the overflow of grace from the obedient response of God's people will reveal a heavenly strategy that always had the whole Earth in view.

CHAPTER 7

Sovereign Choices

I Will Have Mercy

God has the right to make strategic choices among us in order to fulfill His purpose in history; He is the possessor of Heaven and Earth. For example, He had the right to say to Moses, "I will have mercy on whomever I will have mercy, and I will have compassion on whomever I will have compassion" (Romans 9:15).

God's conversation with Moses took place in a tent outside the camp of Israel where He would meet with His servant. Others who also wanted to seek the Lord would go to this "tent of meeting" as well (Exodus 33:7). But God would speak there to Moses as a man speaks to a friend. In fact, when Moses would enter the tent, a pillar of cloud would visibly descend and stand at the tent's door so the people would see the cloud and worship the Lord.

As awesome as it was for Moses to experience God's presence in a cloud, he wanted more; he wanted to see the glory of God (Exodus 33:18). Is there a difference between God's presence and His glory? It would seem so because the Lord began to describe how He would answer Moses' prayer.

Beholding God's Glory

God decided to put Moses in a cleaved rock, and cover him with His hand, but allowed Moses to see His back as He passed by declaring His name and His goodness. When He had moved past Moses, the Lord proclaimed His mercy, compassion, longsuffering and justice. Perhaps we could say that the unveiling of God's glory occurs when His holy nature comes into view as we stand in His presence.

What a precious privilege to gain accurate insight into the nature of God. How we long to behold Him as He really is not just as we think He is, or as our theology informs us He is. Clearly, God is greater than our perception of Him. Imagine seeing God in the flawless expression of absolute purity without mixture of any kind. Such an experience would consume us! Yet God was revealed in such flawless perfection two thousand years ago in Christ. He became a man so that we might behold Him without perishing.

But when Moses asked to see His glory, the Lord's response was simply that He would have mercy and compassion on whomever He wanted. In other words, He was not referring to who would or would not go to Heaven when they died. He was talking about those to whom He would reveal His glory as they stood in His presence in this life.

It's About Mercy

Whenever the Lord reveals Himself in some way to any of His children, He is expressing mercy. It is not as though any of us deserves such an experience. But God's intent is greater than our experience of Him; He wants those around us to be affected by what we have seen. In other words, His mercy on us results in mercy flowing out to others. The reality is that in Moses' day, all of Israel reaped blessing because of God's mercy on him. His strategy remains the same today.

Have you seen something of God's heart for the nations, for your neighborhood, for the poor, for God's people to bear a greater prophetic intercessory heart for the lost, etc.? Have you seen something of His purpose revealed in Scripture? Then you have seen something of His glory; He has had mercy on you. It is not as though you are necessarily more holy, more spiritual, or more mature than others. It is that He has mercy on whomever He decides (Romans 9:16).

Was it because Moses was such a holy man that the Lord decided to speak to him from a burning bush? Or was it rather the initiative and work of God that over many years of trial fashioned Moses into a holy man? How silly we are when we think that there must be something commendable in us motivating God to reveal His glory in some measure to us. Perhaps it was that we fasted a certain amount? Or prayed with a certain intensity? No. He arose in mercy out of His own sovereign purpose, chose each of us and then called us to himself that we might see some dimension of His awesome nature.

It's About the Earth

God even raised up Pharaoh to rule Egypt because He had a plan for His own people that would ultimately release mercy to the nations. If you had asked the Jews of Moses' day why God had raised up this Egyptian leader, many would have probably replied that God wanted him to rule an impressive empire, have a massive army, and make a great name for himself. But they would have misinterpreted God's plan.

> For the Scripture says to the Pharaoh, For this very purpose I have raised you up, that I may show My power in you, and that My name may be declared in all the earth. (Romans 9:17)

Because of what the Lord did to Egypt in delivering His people from bondage, His name became well known throughout that whole part of the world. Nations feared the approaching Israelis and their God. Even today, the story of God's manifest power to rain plagues upon Egypt and to divide the Red Sea is well known throughout the whole Earth.

Many people think that the Bible is primarily about Heaven and hell. I would agree with this assessment for those who do not know the Lord personally. Indeed, those who have never been born anew by the power of the Holy Spirit must face the issue of where they will go when they die. The Bible certainly has the answer for them. But for those who love the Lord and enjoy reading and studying His Word, one truth quickly becomes clear. God's holy book is not only about Heaven. It is also about the Earth and what is emerging from Heaven among us.

For example, He promised that as surely as He lives the whole Earth would not only be filled with His glory, but men would recognize it (Habakkuk 2:14). He then instructed us to pray that His will be done here on Earth as it is in Heaven.

These are not secondary issues. God sent His Son to die and rise again to break the power of sin not only so that we could have heavenly bliss, but so that His Kingdom might break forth and then be extended on the Earth. Most of the Scripture does not have to do with life after death, but with the revelation of God among people in this life.

The Christian life is not about simply going to Heaven, but about living out Heaven's value system in full view of the nations. In fact, God has determined to bring to fullness among the nations a mighty work of the Holy Spirit to reveal the glory of His Son.

The nations must see the glory of Christ. Israel also must see the beauty of their Messiah revealed both individually and corporately in the lives of the redeemed.

Buckle your seat belt. God's glory will be coming more clearly into view in the years ahead.

CHAPTER 8

GOD'S UNSTOPPABLE PURPOSE

An Appointment for Confrontation

When God reveals His glory, He is expressing His mercy not only toward those who behold Him, but also toward those whose lives they touch. Even those who do not believe in the Lord and oppose His people are being given a chance to see His mercy in action.

For example, when Pharaoh opposed Israel's deliverance, God responded to his hardened heart by continuing the hardening process. Notice Paul's words:

'Therefore He has mercy on whom He wills, and whom He wills He hardens" (Romans 9:18).

The Lord had an appointment for confrontation with Pharaoh at the Red Sea. He had decided to make His own name and power known in all the Earth, and He would use Egypt's king to do it.

Many readers of the Scriptures have concluded that the Lord must have wanted to send Pharaoh to hell. But that is not what the Bible necessarily teaches. God put a hook in the jaw of this king and drew him to the Red Sea to establish before men His own reputation; His own glorious name and power would be exalted among the nations.

God's Opposition

When the Egyptians rode on dry ground into the midst of the Red Sea, the Lord arose to trouble them. In the morning watch, a period of several hours stretching from two a.m. until dawn, He caused their chariot wheels to fall off and brought confusion among them so that they could neither move forward nor backward. In the midst of their trouble it began to dawn on them that the God of Israel was opposing them.

> ...and the Egyptians said, "Let us flee from the face of Israel, for the LORD fights for them against the Egyptians." (Exodus 14:25)

The reality of who was opposing them began to weigh very heavily on these men. Maybe they had convinced themselves that the earlier plagues of darkness, frogs, lice, etc., were just coincidences. But now, death was clearly upon them and no matter how they tried, they could not get themselves out of harm's way. God had promised Moses that He would move in such a way that the Egyptians would know it was He who was judging them (Exodus 14:18).

So, did all these soldiers wind up in hell? While many of us might think we know the answer to this question, the truth is that we really do not. God gave them a several hour period of time in which the reality of His power began to dawn on them. As they struggled with their horses, chariots, and weapons, we simply do not know if any, a few, or many cried out to the God of Israel to forgive their opposition to Him and His purpose. If they had humbled themselves in these circumstances and cried out for mercy, would the Lord not have heard and mercifully forgiven them?

The point is that we sometimes tend to make Heaven and hell the main point of a passage of Scripture when what the Lord is talking about is His purpose on Earth.

Present Implications

Even in our own day, the Lord is putting His hook in the jaw of many people to bring them to a confrontation with himself. The reason is because He has purposed that His name would be made known in all the Earth. While mighty and powerful people often think only in terms of their own name, fame, and reputation, the Lord has His own agenda for mankind.

Political, military, and economic leaders might think that they clearly see the goal to which they are leading their nations. And if you asked many of the various media commentators (and maybe even many Christians) why these leaders had come to such international influence, they would probably say that it was to have great authority among men. But they would have misinterpreted God's purpose. The truth is He is doing something among men for the sake of His own glory.

Vessels of Honor and Dishonor

While some individuals have been called to be mere political leaders of nations, others have been called to the much more significant role of beholding the glory of God. From the same lump of worthless clay the Lord has brought forth both vessels of honor and dishonor (Romans 9:21). For example, there was nothing in the clay (i.e., the human nature) of Moses to commend him to God. But the Lord chose him to be a vessel for honor while He called Pharaoh to be but a mere king of an empire.

Moses had the opportunity to be mightily used of the Lord in the revelation of His glory; Pharaoh had the opportunity to learn by experience that resisting God is foolish. Only the Lord really knows whether he ever got the point in this life.

63

Today, God's purpose is moving inexorably toward His goal. Highly influential men and women speak confidently of their plans for the Earth, all the while rejecting the counsel of the Lord as revealed in His Word. If too many children are being born in our nation to accommodate our agenda, then (as in China) we will introduce a one child per couple policy. If pregnancies are too inconvenient to our lifestyle (as in the West), we will simply terminate them. If men want to be physically intimate with other men, we will demand that such activity be seen as normal. Then simply silence through intimidation those who in their consciences do not agree.

But what if God does not agree? Then many will discover that He has set up an appointment with them for confrontation. Wherever you are in the unfolding scenario, make no mistake about it; the Lord will reveal His power and make His name famous throughout the whole Earth. Nothing will stand in His way.

Some people will die rather than admit that they are out of tune with their Creator. Some will cry out to Him in the last minutes of their lives. But others will hear a call to stand before Him and to learn His heart for the nations. As these respond faithfully to the Lord, He will use them in His stated goal of filling the Earth with the knowledge of His glory.

Vessels of Wrath and Mercy

We must never mistake for apathy God's longsuffering endurance of those who brazenly reject His counsel. Vessels headed for wrath are in a process that will culminate in destruction (Romans 9:22). Simultaneously, in the unfolding process, God in His mercy is presently revealing His glory in some measure to others who are learning His ways. God has been preparing these vessels of mercy to both know and express His glory to those around them. Conflict between the two groups is both inevitable and ongoing.

God's merciful redemptive plan for the Earth reveals at the same time His judgments among men. The question each of us must face is whether we will be a living example of the foolishness of saying "no" to God or an illustration of the wisdom of saying "yes." Even those who lived in opposition to the Lord all their lives may in the last minutes of their existence find the grace to repent and be forgiven, for instance, the thief on the cross. Of course, the Scripture does not hold out to be emulated either his or Pharaoh's lifestyle choices.

But let us not miss the point. The truth to be proclaimed in the midst of the ongoing great spiritual war is the splendor of the One who has called us to behold His glory.

PART TWO

ILLUMINATING THE NATIONS

"In Him was life, and the life was the light of men."

John 1:4

CHAPTER 9

AN INCREASING REVELATION

God's Gracious Persistence

God has determined to reveal His glory throughout the whole Earth. Even though the defeated enemy of our souls keeps up his war of attrition and desperately tries to change the subject, the Lord will not be deterred. He keeps arising among unworthy people and calling forth from the nations both vessels of honor and dishonor. To one group He will continue to reveal His power in the demonstration of His wrath because of their ongoing obstinate opposition to Him. To the other, He is mercifully giving insight into His own heart and purpose for the nations. But through it all, God himself and His activity lie at the heart of the great spiritual conflict of the ages continuing to unfold before our eyes. The Lord, not man is at the center of world history.

But how will all this end? And to what degree will God's glory and beauty be made known among men before He comes in final devastating and eternal judgments at the end of history?

Notice Paul's thoughts concerning the vessels of mercy called by God from among both the Jews and the Gentiles.

As He says also in Hosea: I will call them My people, who were not My people, and her beloved, who was not beloved. And it shall come to pass in the place where it was said to them, 'You are not My people,' there they shall be called sons of the living God. (Romans 9:25, 26)

The Lord would call His own those who were never known as His people and He would do so right in the nations where they lived. Instead of people having to make pilgrimage to a holy temple in Jerusalem in order to meet with God, He intended to arise and reveal His glory simply everywhere. Vessels of mercy would be found in the remotest parts of the Earth.

Present Revelation

This display of Heaven's mercy is occurring today not because people deserve salvation. Rather, God is making himself known among men to fulfill His own promise to fill the Earth with the knowledge of His glory. As surely as He lives, He is keeping His promise.

But has He fully achieved what He set out to do? Or are there yet many millions of people, called by God from the foundation of the world to be vessels of mercy, but who have not yet come to know Him? I submit to you that indeed many will be turning to the Lord in the years ahead; there is yet a fullness to come from among the Gentile nations of the Earth.

Such fullness has to do with more than simply the numbers of people involved. Rather, what God wants to make known are the various insights into His own heart and purpose that He will be revealing to each one.

God has much to say yet about himself. Even though the canon of Scripture has been completed, the Lord continues to reveal himself during the Church age by the power of the Holy Spirit. What He unveils of himself is always in harmony with the Bible; He never contradicts His Word. But the days of heavenly revelation are far from over.

For example, if the believers in first century Ephesus needed among them not only the spirit of wisdom, but also of revelation in the knowledge of God (Ephesians 1:17), then certainly we do today as well. God has made and continues to make available to us the greatest source of eternal wealth. That limitless well of living water is none other than God himself. If the treasures of wisdom and knowledge are hidden in the person of Christ, should we not be spending time with Him, searching the recesses of His heart? (Colossians 2:2-3) Has He not given us His Holy Spirit whose nature it is to plumb the depths of God? "But God has revealed them to us through His Spirit. For the Spirit searches all things, yes, the deep things of God" (1 Corinthians 2:10).

If we are responding appropriately to His Spirit, we will be moving with Him into those depths. This brings us to the greatest questions facing our generation: Is the God of Heaven and Earth coming into greater clarity among us? Is He making known and are we learning His motives, desires, and priorities? Remember, Moses was not content to only see His power and to experience His presence. Rather, when given the opportunity, he wanted to see God's glory as well.

Our Message

Simply stated, the glory of God made known is the God of glory as He really is, coming into greater clarity to us as we stand in His presence. As He does so, our misconceptions of Him are exposed and adjusted.

This is the message that the nations desperately need to hear; we must preach Him (Galatians 1:16). Paul didn't simply preach *about* Christ; his words carried the presence of the One to whom he was referring. God made himself known through Paul's words. Likewise, the Lord's Word today must bring an impartation of God through us to others. But apart from sovereign intervention, He can only accomplish the accurate,

71

though partial, revelation of himself to the nations through those to whom He has revealed His glory.

The glory of God made known through a people! God, coming into clarity before the nations! Such a theme stuns us. But has not the Lord called us to follow in the footsteps of Jesus? God's purpose in sending His Son among us was to make himself known. And Christ revealed the Father perfectly. Since Jesus was God put into human terms, no one other than He could have accomplished such a mission.

Yet, we find before us the impossible task of making known to the nations the glory of the One who has sent us. Has God indeed called us to such a work? Yes. The reason He prepares vessels of mercy is to make known the riches of His glory upon them to the nations (Romans 9:23).

Because of His Mercy

But what is His glory upon us? It is His love, His forgiveness, His compassion, His hatred of sin, and so on (Exodus 34:6-7). It can be so easy to get the message mixed up and begin to think that it is about us. God takes what we see as we stand before Him and begins to work it into the fiber of our beings. We literally partake of His divine nature (2 Peter 1:4), and start experiencing what He feels about the poor, the lost, the subject of abortion, how His house should be built, etc.

As a result, His burdens become ours. Others will hear what we say and watch how we live and identify the burden of the Lord as ours. We then become known as that person who has a heart for Israel, or who has a desire to minister to the poor in the Philippines, or who is always talking about the centrality of Christ in the Church, etc. But if we are ministering accurately, what we are expressing is actually the contents of His heart.

Then as we each live in harmony with His unique calling on our lives, those around us will see in some measure the glory of God upon us. And it is all because He has had mercy on us.

The result is that the nations begin experiencing God as He really is, slowly coming into view. Notice, it is not our glory and fame that is the message. God's theme is not about us, about our successes in ministry, or about our wisdom in building something for Him.

We are not vessels of excellence, or of intellectual greatness, or of philosophical sophistication. We are vessels of mercy. God has brought us all forth from the dust of the ground, and we all deserve His wrath. But for the sake of the Earth and for fulfilling His own promise, He has had mercy on many and revealed himself to them in some measure.

The question now before us is whether or not He is content with the measure of His glory now made known to the nations. Or is there more to be revealed?

I submit that there is a degree of fullness yet to be unveiled among the nations. The reason is because Israel continues on in her existence without an intimate knowledge of her Messiah. And the apostle clearly stated that:

> ...blindness in part has happened to Israel until the fullness of the Gentiles has come in. And so all Israel will be saved. (Romans 11:25, 26)

> Lord, arise and reveal your glory in greater and clearer ways to us and through us. Arise and bring to fullness the unveiling of your beauty among the nations in these days. And bring Israel to the knowledge of her Messiah. In Jesus' name, Amen.

CHAPTER 10

A PERVADING DEATH

A Coming Sign

Is the increase of God's glory among the nations really the primary focus of Heaven during the Church age? If so, what are the implications for His Church? And what about Israel?

It seems that Paul made conflicting statements about his Jewish nation. First he said that even if Israel were numbered as the sand of the sea, only a remnant would be saved (Romans 9:27). Then he stated that when the fullness of the Gentiles comes in, all Israel would be saved (Romans 11:26). So which is it?

Since God would not contradict himself, both statements are obviously true. When Christ came two thousand years ago, Israel did not receive Him. Though they had indeed become as numerous as the stars and the sand (Hebrews 11:12) there was only a remnant that believed and was saved (Romans 11:5). By and large, His own did not receive Him, but as many as did so, to them He gave the right to become children of God (John 1:11, 12).

But as Church history continues to progress, God is indeed bringing to fullness His work in His redeemed people among the nations.[3] And when He has fully produced that for which He has sent His Holy Spirit in order to get Israel's attention, then her eyes will be opened, she will become jealous, and she will turn back to her God.

What a sign to the nations when God reveals himself to Israel! What rejoicing in Heaven! What grief in hell!

Israel—Key to God's Plan

One main reason that Satan has inspired anti-Semitism in so many places, for so many years, is because he knows that the Jews are key in God's plan for world redemption. Do you remember Jesus' words to the woman at the well? He told her that while her people did not really know what they were worshiping, the Jews did. Then He uttered a most startling statement. He said, "...Salvation is of the Jews" (John 4:22).

Just think about it. Today we have the Bible because of God's interaction with the Jews. When He sent His Son to die for the sins of the world, He sent Him to Israel. Sin and hell were defeated at Calvary outside the city gates of the Jews' capital city. Then after Jesus rose from the dead, He ascended to Heaven from Mount Olivet, a mere Sabbath day's journey from that same city (Acts 1:12).

All the saving work of God among men can be traced back to events occurring in the Jewish nation two thousand years ago. Even their rejection of their Messiah could not prevent the greater work of God to bring His salvation to the nations of the Earth. In fact, He turned to the nations to make Israel jealous!

Wealth for the World

Paul stated that Israel's fall brought riches for the world. What

---

3   Since the Jews have returned to their own land, they are now one of those nations. In Israel there is a growing band of Messianic believers in whom God is arising to reveal His glory.

wealth—The forgiveness of sins, God's holy presence dwelling in the hearts of His people, His wisdom made known within them, the hope of eternal life, etc.

But the apostle also holds out for us an amazing expectation. Even though riches were realized through Israel's fall, much more will be apprehended through her coming into her fullness (Romans 11:12). The overflow of God's salvation that has come to the nations through Israel's failure two thousand years ago has been an amazing blessing to the world. Think of all the individuals who have been born of the Holy Spirit, or of those who have been healed supernaturally in their bodies, or of the hospitals and orphanages started by believing men and women. Think of the schools and universities built by Christians to help educate many. The list could go on and on.[4]

But Paul says that much more will be realized when Israel comes back to her God. In fact, he informs us that the nations will experience life from the dead (Romans 11:15). His use of the words, "life from the dead" echoes back to earlier in this letter where he tells us that as believers we are now alive from the dead (Romans 6:13). In other words, Paul seems to be referring to the rebirth experience.

Can we really expect that God will release among the nations through Israel's salvation a much greater expression of His saving and redeeming power than has been experienced over the last two thousand years? I believe we must. Remember Jesus' statement that salvation is of the Jews.

Israel's Salvation–Implications

Such thinking has major implications as the Church looks toward the years ahead. Many Christians seem to think only in

---

4   It is also true that there have been times when sins of arrogance, moral failure, and lust for political power, etc., have marred the Church's record. But without God's people, the world would be a much darker place.

terms of escape from coming darkness and tribulation. But God has a plan to make His glory known in ways greater than He has in the past.

Earlier in his letter to the Romans, Paul stated that much more than to whatever degree death came through Adam, God's grace and His gift of righteousness flourished to many people. In fact, much more than however much death reigned or *called the shots* among men because of Adam, those who received the abundance of grace and of the gift of righteousness would reign in life through Christ (Romans 5:15-17).

What a promise. He would have a people who rule more in life because of Christ than death ruled because of Adam. This begs a question: How much has death reigned among men? First there was the spiritual death brought about from Adam's sin. Then from that we see physical death quickly manifest in Cain's murder of his brother. From there we go on to read of mankind's history filled with wars, greed, political intrigue, etc. We see people because of their personal decisions, reaping relational death, financial death, emotional death, as well as physical death, and so on.

But God has decreed that those who learn to receive the abundance of God's grace and of the gift of His righteousness will live lives of victorious ruling more than death has! Do we yet see the Christian Church living at such a level of spiritual victory? Death continues to harass the nations of the Earth and even the people of God with seeming invincibility.

Death: Still Operating

Today we see death *calling the shots* in the lives of many among America's youth. We look at our political establishment and see the pervading sense of spiritual death in the priorities of many leaders. We also see death invading the relational commitments among many married couples when they fall to the temptation to commit adultery.

Not only that, we see death and its influences in God's house as well. When His children choose to harbor bitterness rather than to forgive those who have hurt them, they choose death over life. Christian couples do so as well when they tear from each other and dissolve their marital covenants. Church splits, men promoting their ministries more than Christ, leaders seeking money rather than souls—these all testify to the presence of death in the one place on Earth where life is supposed to be the distinguishing factor.

But all the psychological counseling and psychotropic drugs in the world are useless when combating the insidious creeping influence of this seemingly universal enemy of God released on Earth through Adam thousands of years ago.

What is the answer to this? Is there good news to be found in the midst of all the bad?

Very simply, we must learn to receive both the abundance of God's grace and the gift of His righteousness in order to reign. Grace to forgive others; grace to serve those to whom He sends us, grace to homeschool our children, grace to prophesy, etc. The list goes on and on.

Whatever tasks He puts in our hands to do, we must humble ourselves to receive His grace to accomplish. And when we fail, we must learn to quickly repent and receive His wonderful gift of righteousness. Don't wallow in guilt at your failures; quickly turn and embrace God's offer.

How long does it take for you to receive His forgiveness when you fail? Do you feel it necessary to do some sort of penance before you are again in full fellowship with Him? To whatever degree we hesitate to receive what is freely offered, to that degree we fail to reign.

Lord, help us to believe your good news to us, for it is your power unto salvation. Help us to receive the abundance of your grace and the abundance of your gift of righteousness that we might live in intimacy with you. Forgive us when we live more in harmony with spiritual death than we do with your life, present in us. In Jesus' name. Amen.

CHAPTER 11

THE DEATH OF DEATH

❦

The Presence of Death

Today we see the pervading influence of death among the nations, even infecting the Church. At the same time, Israel is simply not jealous either of us or of the ways in which our faith is made visible. Is God's plan in trouble? Sometimes, it seems like it is.

Times of revival are accompanied not only by many people being filled with the Holy Spirit, but also by many churches being severely shaken. Sinful attitudes surface, believers split from one another, and the testimony of God is undermined. Yet at the same time, new churches are also planted and many people are born again and filled with God's Spirit. The problem however, is that even though our numbers are growing, the world sees a muddled Christianity rather than a pure expression of God's glory. In other words, even in the exhilarating times of the outpourings of His life, we still find death actively and visibly at work among God's own people.

One thing is clear as we gaze across the spiritual landscape;

mixture abounds in the Lord's house. We need a breakthrough.
The Lord promised that His Kingdom would grow slowly as
would a seed into a large tree. And it has. But He also promised
that however much wealth would be released to the nations
through Israel's fall, much more would be realized through her
salvation. What could the "much more" possibly be?

Paul stated that a partial hardening had come upon Israel,
but only for a season. When the fullness of the Gentiles came
in, all Israel would be saved. At that time, the nations would
experience life from the dead (Romans 11:15). Could the phrase
"life from the dead" indicate more than simply a sudden increase
in the number of believers? Could God also be planning a
breakthrough against the power of death and to further deliver
the nations from its influence prior to its final defeat at the
resurrection?

God's Strategy: A Feast

Isaiah spoke of a time when the Lord would make for all people
on the mountain of the Lord, a feast of choice pieces and aged
wine (Isaiah 25:6). The Hebrew word for choice pieces is
SHEMEN, which is translated as oil in Exodus 30:25, 26, where
it refers to the holy anointing oil.

A feast of oil and aged wine! If oil and wine speak of the
joy, presence, and anointing of the Holy Spirit, then God must
want us to feast upon His presence in His holy mountain of
Zion. The New Testament teaches that we have presently come
to Zion in the gathering of Christ's church (Hebrews 12:22-24).

Perhaps it is time for us to reconsider our ways and see
that God views our gatherings as feasts. When we assemble to
worship and pray, we are to feast upon Him by simply coming
to Him in faith (John 6:31–35). We are to also feast upon Him
in the Lord's Supper (which should probably be taken in the
context of a meal together. After all, Scripture does refer to
it as a supper, not a snack (1 Corinthians 11:17-30, Jude 12).

Of course, we are to feast upon Him in His Word (Matthew 4:4, Ezekiel 2:8–3:3). And finally, we are to feast by doing the specific works He has given us to accomplish (John 4:34).

But if our times together are not permeated with the oil and the wine, then they will cease to be feasts and simply become times of mere religious formalism.

Consuming Death

God has made an amazing promise. As His people begin attending His appointed feast, He will do something miraculous for the nations of the Earth.

> And He will destroy {Hebrew, BALA—to swallow up} on this mountain the surface of the covering cast over all people, and the veil that is spread over all nations. He will swallow up death forever, and the Lord GOD will wipe away tears from all faces; the rebuke of His people He will take away from all the earth; for the LORD has spoken. (Isaiah 25:7, 8)

The key to changing the Earth will not be found as churches assemble to form new strategies in order to bring change to their respective nations. Rather, change will come when God's people submit to His plan and cease from all our good intentions and ideas. God has His own strategy. It is that we make Christ the focus of our lives and of our times together and simply gather unto Him as the true Bread of Heaven. Isaiah informs us that as we do so, God himself will swallow up death's international veil. He will do so specifically from the locale of His Mountain where His people have gathered to His feast.

He promised that as we feast upon Him, He will then feast upon (i.e., swallow up) death and its influence over the nations. A great breakthrough against the effects of death permeating the nations lies in our future, if we will but arise from where we are and attend God's feast.

Obviously, death will not be totally destroyed until the time of the resurrection (1 Corinthians 15:26, 54). However, the New Testament also indicates that death's defeat has already begun and is well underway (2 Timothy 1:10; Hebrews 2:14, 15). But we must take ground in our day against its continuing operations.

Speaking of Life; Imparting Death

The question we face is whether our times together are feasts or funerals. Funerals are events where life is talked about but death is prominently displayed. Too often, Christian meetings are like that. We can fill our times together with talk about Christ and at the same time display the attributes of death. Pride, self-promotion, envy, political manipulation, unforgiving attitudes, etc., all reveal man's priorities rather than God's. But Christ, His life, and His priorities are to be what distinguishes us.

Someone once said that if a speaker has the measles and lectures others on the dangers of contracting the flu, the listeners may become experts on the flu, even writing down many notes concerning the dangers of this sickness. Yet while possessing great knowledge of the flu's signs, symptoms, aftereffects, etc., the speaker will have infected them with the measles. Talking about one thing, imparting something else—herein lays a great danger for us in Christ's Church. We can actually be part of the problem of death's influence in our particular nation.

Jesus himself is life. He must become practically for each of us our sustenance, and our nourishment. We cannot settle for mere religious formalism. We must recognize that apart from His manifest presence in our lives and in our gatherings, we will die. And we will contribute to the work of death in our nation even while talking about Christ.

All Are Welcome

We must invite the lost. Notice that all people are invited to this great meal (Isaiah 25:6). Here is our message to this generation: come celebrate the resurrection of God's Son. He invites all to receive the forgiveness of their sins and to feast at His great dinner.

Two thousand years ago, Jesus likened His Kingdom to a man hosting a great supper that many would rather be excused from than attend (Luke 14:15–24). Finally, after hearing the excuses, the host told his servants to *compel* people to come in so that his house may be filled.

God is so committed to filling His house of feasting that He will resort to compelling grace in order to do so. While I do believe that our human will is involved in our salvation experience, it is also true that sometimes God can be quite insistent that people turn to Him. Saul of Tarsus seems to be one example of God's intense invitation method. While Saul certainly exercised his will to some degree when he turned to Christ, yet it is also clear that it would have been difficult for him to resist a light brighter than the midday sun and the Lord's audible voice calling him by name.

In the Old Testament, Jonah also found the compelling grace of God would not let him go where he wanted. By the way, have you found yourself on any free fish rides lately?

No matter how you look at it, God's goal for His people will not be realized by human initiatives but by His ingenuity and sovereign commitment. His house will be filled and it will be known for the feast going on inside.

To sum up our thoughts so far, the Lord will accomplish a work in His people in order to make Israel jealous. Then when the Jewish nation turns to Him, the nations of the Earth will experience what Paul refers to as "life from the dead." God's strategy is that as His people learn to feast upon His Son, He will turn and intensify His ongoing destruction of death and its influence among the nations, bringing us ultimately to death's final demise at the resurrection.

I submit to you that the call of God is sounding forth in our day. "Come attend the feast I have prepared for you."

I also submit to you that when Israel turns back to God, He will at that time arise in new dimensions of compelling grace in order to see His house filled. As we used to sing some years ago in some sections of the Lord's feast: "Multitudes are coming can't you hear the sound and we're just standing on the edge of the rain."

CHAPTER 12

THE TRIUMPH OF LIFE

God's Life

God intends for His people to so receive the abundance of His grace and His righteousness, that we would reign in life more than death has reigned through Adam's sin (Romans 5:17). In other words, He intends to shape the world by the power of His life within His people prior to the return of Christ more than death has.[5] The Lord's goal is nothing less than a people filled and overflowing with His life, and living accordingly.

Jesus Christ is our example. The conclusion we draw from observing His earthly ministry is that after all was said and done, His life conquered death (John 2:19; 1 Corinthians 15:12-20). Christ's resurrection makes this compelling proclamation; God's life is more powerful than death and it triumphs over death.

And it is His life that has been poured into His people. Believers do not simply talk about God; we have His very presence in our hearts (Romans 8:9). He is as much on Earth

---

5   Paul's theme of receiving the abundance of God's grace and the gift of His righteousness clearly has to do with the Church age prior to Christ's return.

today through the presence of the Holy Spirit as He was through the incarnation of Christ two thousand years ago. The Holy Spirit is not some portion of the deity; He is not one third of God. The Creator of Heaven and Earth is present on Earth dwelling in a people. This reality is what defines Christianity.

We have simply lost our way if we allow ourselves to be defined by the buildings we meet in, the Christian leaders we relate to, the evangelistic methods we use, the doctrines we hold to,[6] etc. The house of God is to be known primarily for one thing—God lives there. And where God lives, death has no future.

Victorious Life

All of us want to see the light of God increase among the nations. How the world needs illumination! Even though the Lord has called His Church to this task, the world is filled with darkness. Why? The answer lies in the fact that it is not religion but life that illuminates the souls of men. In Christ was life and that life was the light of men (John 1:4). Jesus, filled with the life of His Father, stepped into a world of great darkness and proceeded to turn on the lights (Isaiah 9:1-2; Matthew 4:13-17). In fact, while He was on Earth, He was the only source of spiritual light available for the whole planet (John 9:5).

But as the light began to dawn two thousand years ago in the nation of Israel, those more involved in a religion about God than they were with God himself, rose up to extinguish that light. Remarkably, John's two-fold testimony some years later was that the darkness never really did comprehend what the light was all about, and that the same light continued to shine on Earth even after Jesus had gone back to Heaven (John 1:5).

Today, the light persists in the nations through the lives of God's people. Even if it is somewhat dim compared to how it

6 This is not to imply that proper teaching and understanding of Christian doctrine is unimportant; it is crucial. But let us not gather to mere teaching, but to Him who would open His Word to us.

shone in Christ two thousand years ago, that light continues to get brighter. The Lord has a declaration to make: "My life, which is the light of men, conquers death!"

The great spiritual conflict today remains between life and death. And that war is being fought not only in the world, but also in the house of God. Religion is the counterfeit of life. It illuminates nothing and produces death. On the other hand, God's life illuminates the human soul and exposes death for what it is.

As a result, the religious spirit hates and opposes the life of God, and seeks to crush it in the hearts of people. Even as the religious spirit in Israel sought to extinguish the light in Christ, so also throughout Church history it has sought to extinguish the same light in faithful believers among the nations.

But the life of God will triumph and His power to illuminate the darkened souls of men will increasingly be released as His people come to live consistently in harmony with Christ, alive in us.

The Road of Life

Above all else, the Church is about Christ, and He is our life (John 14:6). Unfortunately, many who once believed and came to deeply love the Lord Jesus have lost their way. In losing sight of Him, they have lost the road of life. Jesus is both the road to life and the road of life.[7] Just as the road leading to life was narrow, and there were few finding it two thousand years ago (Matthew 7:14) the road of life once found must not then be taken for granted. We must continually seek and discover Christ in the daily experiences of the Christian life.

The enemy seeks to obscure Christ from our sight. Satan doesn't mind us filling our lives with Christian terminology, many meetings and activities, even supporting our choices with

---

7   Jesus said He was both the way and the life (John 14:6). The word "way" in Greek is HODOS meaning a road. Therefore He is both the road by which life is found and He is the life to be enjoyed while on the road.

Christian doctrine, as long as the person of Christ doesn't fill those activities. The Christian life can so easily become an empty shell. If Christ doesn't permeate our Christian experience, we then settle for a lifestyle that over time will cloud our eyes from beholding Him. In fact, those very activities will take His place. How subtle the enemy is.

Whatever then takes God's place in His own house becomes a false god. But false gods have no staying power. While they may abide for many years in the Church, yet when God arises, they crumble before Him and the road of life is again revealed. But such awakenings bring opposition from those who have grown comfortable with the status quo.

The Ongoing Clash

Clearly, the great spiritual war between life and death must be won in the Church. Life must triumph over death among us if it is ever to bring the kind of change that God intends for the nations.

Today much of the Church is literally powerless before the suffocating veil of spiritual death afflicting the nations. The reason is because too many of us find our identities in the Christian life rather than in Christ who *is* our life. But if we would humble ourselves before Him and consistently receive from Him the abundance of both His grace and His righteousness, we would then find the beauty of His holy character and purpose filling our vision.

Worship would then spring up from our hearts and we would become thankful for all He has done and continues to do in us. Faith would rise up in our hearts expecting Him to reveal himself in even the seemingly mundane experiences of daily life. Illumination would come to our souls and would then filter out to those around us who think that darkness is light and that life without God is normal.

But what is usual is not necessarily normal. Two thousand years ago, the only normal man to walk the Earth *stepped up to the plate* and announced that those who had seen Him had seen God. (It took God to be a man and reveal normalcy.) The light of God began to shine and many who enjoyed the darkness reacted quite negatively. But God had promised something through the prophet Isaiah. The light would dawn in Israel and would slowly increase among the nations (Isaiah 60:1-7). Even kings would come to the rising light. And what would be God's objective? He would beautify and make glorious His house (vs. 7, 13, 14).

Today, the war for the soul of the nations is being fought in the Church. And most do not seem to understand the issues. The light that illuminates the world is found only in the life of God. We must return to Him with all of our hearts and be filled with His life. Our gatherings must become feasts of life. The living presence of God must become our focus. Christian leadership cannot change the world. Apostles cannot change the world. But a people filled with life will shine and the nations will be confronted with the light that exposes delusions.

92

CHAPTER 13

DEVOTED TO LIFE

The Destruction of Division

Two thousand years ago, Christ took into His own flesh the enmity—the bitter attitudes between Jew and Gentile —and forever obliterated them at the Cross. In that hour, He abolished the Law of Moses as the environment for Jew/Gentile relationships so that in himself He might create one new man made up of both groups (Ephesians 2:14-16). Up until that time, the law was the environment for those relationships. If Gentiles wanted to have any real lasting intimacy with the Jewish people, they had to be circumcised and keep the Law of Moses.

The Church—Organization or Miraculous Organism

But when the Savior of the world established the foundation of His Kingdom by defeating sin and death at Calvary, He himself then became the environment for relational intimacy for all His people. It is as we are immersed into Him and then learn to abide in Him that we come to love one another as God has loved us. Such love is the proof of our identity as learners of Christ (John 15, 13:35).

As we look at the Church, can it be said that we have proven to the world that we are learning Christ? Do we see emerging among the nations Paul's "one new man" made up of many diverse parts yet revealing one mind, the mind of Christ (Ephesians 4:13; 1 Corinthians 2:16)? The Church is supposed to be a miraculous entity, an organism not an organization.

It is exactly here on this issue that the war between life and death for the soul of the nations is being fought. If we do not understand and apply properly the truth both of what the Church is and how she is to function, how will God's light ever illuminate the world's way forward? How can the nations walk in the light of God's city if we do not know what it means to be God's city and then live accordingly?

Sharing Life

There can be no illumination for this dark world if the Church continues to be defined by anything other than God's life. Jewish life, Caucasian life, Asian life, African life—none of these are the basis for building God's house. And yet many search for biblical justification for walking separately from others in Christ based on human ethnicity.

We must repent. Our common life is the life of God. Fellowship (Greek, KOINONIA) means the sharing of a common life. We must spend time together sharing His life with each other. We have often confused social interaction with fellowship. But they are not the same thing. If unbelievers can have the same social experience among themselves as we do as believers in our times together, then we have simply settled for social interaction among ourselves. Interacting socially with one another is good. But we must not confuse it with the miraculous experience of sharing God's life with each other. Without such communication, there simply is no illumination occurring in our conversations.

When I plan to get together with other believers, I pray and ask that the Lord will manifest His life in our discussions. Why? The answer is that His life is the light of men, and I need to see more clearly than I do. Not only that, I want to help those in darkness to also see the light of life. Without the experience of supernaturally empowered fellowship, the local church becomes no different as far as illuminating their locale than the local tavern, even if the believers are faithfully canvassing their area with door-to-door evangelistic campaigns.

We desperately need the manifestation of God's life among us. We need Him to fill our teachings, our exhortations, our singing, etc.

A Devoted People

The early Church was devoted to fellowship (Acts 2:42).

The fact that today so many Christians interpret this verse to mean that the early believers simply enjoyed spending time together is one main reason why the darkness continues to encroach upon and within our nation. In too many cases, we simply don't get it.

We do not know how to do church. The fact that we think we do, reveals why we do not cry out in desperation to Him that He would come and fill our conversation times together with His life.

The early Church was devoted to prayer.

How about corporate prayer among us? So many find prayer meetings to be boring. In many cases, I would have to agree with their assessment. By and large, believers do not know how to flow together in life when praying. So one person drones on and on trying to cover everything he can think of, while others take a short nap and wonder why they are so carnal. "Why can't I get excited about talking to God with others?"

But if we could learn to pray more accurately, according to the flow of God's life among us, we would then find ourselves actually praying the prayers of God. The voice of the Great High Priest who ever lives to intercede for us would be found sounding forth on Earth through the lips of His people. Intercession is not about getting God to take action according to our desires. It is about joining Him in His strategy to extend His Kingdom in all the Earth.

The early Church was devoted to apostolic teaching.

At that point in the Church's history, the apostles were twelve men who were known primarily for one thing—they had spent time with Jesus. The key element then in their on-going apostolic ministries would have to be that they continued to spend time with Him.

To view the sending of the twelve as only a one-time event would be to grossly underestimate the necessity of Christ's ongoing involvement in their lives. Just as Jesus spent consistent time with the Father while on Earth, these men who followed His example were known for spending consistent time with Christ (Acts 6:4). Jesus was constantly sending these men into trying circumstances both locally as well as in other cities. To be an apostle, one sent on a mission, was to be actively involved with the God of Heaven, and then to be regularly dispatched by Him into strategic relational situations.

So when they arrived, what did they teach? They preached Christ.

But when it pleased God…to reveal His Son in me, that I might preach Him. (Galatians 1:15, 16)

Christ in you, the hope of glory. Him we preach. (Colossians 1:27, 28)

When Paul came to Corinth, he determined to know nothing

among them except Christ and Him crucified (1 Corinthians 2:2). In this verse Paul did not say He preached Christ crucified; he said he knew Him crucified. And yet the context of this verse is Paul's preaching. What he taught came out of an intimacy that perceived Christ not only in His resurrection life, but also in His crucifixion. To know Him in such a way meant that Paul experienced suffering and yet found Christ in the midst of it. Then when he spoke, he demonstrated the power and presence of the One who had both sent him into that suffering and also then ministered to him there.

In other words, Paul's words were words of life. They conveyed the life of God so that spiritual illumination came to men's souls. No wonder the powers of darkness got so peeved. To be devoted to the apostles' teaching meant that the disciples were devoted to life.

Finally, the early Church was devoted to the breaking of bread.

If we equate the breaking of bread with simply sharing meals together, we will fail to see darkness arrested. Remember, it is God's life that is the light of men. Our times together must be filled with His life.

Evangelistic efforts will never have the impact that God desires if the local churches from which such endeavors emanate are not regularly experiencing God's manifest life corporately.

If fellowship, the genuine sharing together of God's life then permeates our church suppers, then it will be easy to see the Lord integrate His supper into those times.

Lord, have mercy on your people. Hear our cries to you that you would arise among us, revealing your life in our times together. As we feed upon you as the Bread of Heaven, go forth devouring the veil of death oppressing our land. In Jesus' name. Amen.

CHAPTER 14

GOD'S GLORIOUS HOUSE

A Dawning Light

God's objective is a beautiful and glorious house, filled with His glory. Many years before Christ's incarnation, God promised Israel that though great darkness would cover the Earth, yet His glory would dawn on them (Isaiah 60). Sure enough, many years of darkness ensued among the nations as first the Babylonians, then the Persians, followed by the Greeks under Alexander, and finally the Romans conquered that part of the world. But into the midst of Roman oppression a light began to rise.

> The people who sat in darkness have seen a great light, and upon those who sat in the region and shadow of death Light has dawned. From that time Jesus began to preach and to say, "Repent, for the kingdom of heaven is at hand." (Matthew 4:16, 17)

The emerging light was none other than Christ himself. Over the last two thousand years, kings and nations have turned toward Christ, Israel's light, just as Isaiah prophesied. Then God gave Isaiah further insight. In a time when Israel's sons would be returning to their own land, the nation's eyes would suddenly be opened and they would see and become radiant (Isaiah 60:4, 5). Today, while we see many Jews returning to their homeland, we still await the fulfillment of the promised opening of the nation's eyes; Israel's salvation lies yet in our future.

God's Objective

Isaiah prophesied that great blessings would follow Israel's return to the Lord, resulting in Him achieving His primary objective. He would beautify His glorious house (Isaiah 60:7, 13, 14).

There is a greater glory yet to be revealed in God's house than what we have experienced to this day. According to the Apostle Paul, it hinges upon a certain fullness of the Holy Spirit's work in His Church among the nations so as to make Israel jealous (Romans 11). In this book, we have proposed that God's objective is a growing escalation of the nature and character of Christ in His people. In the end, it will be the Lord Jesus revealing himself in His redeemed people who will win Israel to himself.[8]

It is only then when the fullness of the Gentiles comes in, that all Israel will be saved. This amazing event will then release among the nations greater riches than what came through Israel's fall (Romans 11:12). Along this line, Peter prophesied to the men of Israel that prior to Christ's return when the nation turned back to God, seasons of refreshing would come from the presence of the Lord (Acts 3:19, 20).

In those coming days, God's house will be a place of feasting. Christ himself will be central among us; He will be our life. A growing illumination among the nations will accompany God's

---

8   This is not to deny or draw attention away from the sovereign outpouring of the Holy Spirit that Israel will experience in that day (Zechariah 12:10).

work of devouring the international veil of death shrouded over the world. Many will turn to God.

The result will ultimately be a glorious bride made ready for the Lord. Because of abundant mercy and amazing grace, she will look like she belongs next to Him.

There will also arise in those days a desperate counterattack by Satan as he realizes that his time is short. He will probably take his final stand by pushing for a one-world governmental system rallying around one main goal—the destruction of God's people. But God has him in His crosshairs.

God's Final Environment For Us

God's final Word to the nations is Christ; He is the Word made flesh.

> God, after He spoke long ago to the fathers in the prophets in many portions and in many ways, in these last days has spoken to us in His Son. (Hebrews 1:1, 2 NASB)

The reason that the last days consist of the entire Church age is because God has revealed the final environment for His voice to be heard among men. There can be no days of greater finality; God has found the perfect setting for revealing himself, even His own Son. Our response must be to love the Lord Jesus with all of our hearts and seek to abide in Him. As the Church comes to learn her proper abode, we will find the last days culminating in the last day—the day of Christ's glorious appearing.

Two thousand years ago when the Eternal One became a man and walked among us, eternity tore the fabric of time. Since those days, whenever the Lord pours out His Spirit among us on Earth, the fabric of time shreds a little more. Eternity is busting in on man's plans and agendas, and there is nothing he can do about it except to bow his knee and submit. Getting mad won't help. Rebellion will only bring destruction.

But God informs us that in this era of finality, He has an order, an administration for culminating human history. This divine arrangement of His people is greater than any Christian sect or any organized expression of Christian religion. What God is constructing among us by His Spirit supersedes all the various lines of division presently separating us.

> He made known to us the mystery of His will, according to His kind intention which He purposed in Him with a view to an administration suitable to the fullness of the times, that is, the summing up of all things in Christ, things in the heavens and things on the earth. (Ephesians 1:9, 10 NASB)

God's administration for revealing the mysteries of eternity is simply Christ and all who are alive in Him. And there in this environment, in His Son, God intends to sum up everything that He has been doing since the beginning. In His summation, He will make reference to those in Christ who are in Heaven as well as those still alive on Earth. But if we want to understand His concluding remarks to the creation with any degree of clarity while still on this side of eternity, we must be one of those living and abiding in Christ.

God's Final Remarks To The Nations

Think of someone delivering an important speech. At the end, he summarizes what he has been saying. In other words, he goes back and recapitulates his previous major points, touching on them briefly one more time. While it may have taken a few hours to deliver his word from beginning to end, the recap will be short in comparison. But it will consist of "in a nutshell" the heart of all that he said earlier.

Consider what God has been saying since Adam's days in the Garden of Eden. He has spoken personally to individuals such as Abraham and brought them into their eternal destiny. He spoke in a cloud to Moses of His plans for the nation of Israel. He confronted Egypt's gods with plagues, revealing His power and their bankruptcy. He spoke with revelatory power again and again to the prophets throughout the whole Old Testament era.

And don't forget Elisha's servant who saw the mountains filled with chariots of fire or the false prophets of Baal who saw God's prophet call down holy fire to consume the sacrifice. And then there were the angelic visitations that many experienced, including Daniel, Mary the mother of Jesus, and John on the Isle of Patmos.

Of course, God revealed himself in Christ when He turned water into wine, healed the sick, walked on water, and cast out demons. Since rising from the dead, He has spoken frequently to men and women throughout the last two thousand years. We think of the apostles Peter, Paul, and John. We also acknowledge Madam Guyon, Martin Luther, John Calvin, and the many heroes of the faith in the last century, etc.

Clearly, the Lord has been speaking and revealing His purpose among men through many mighty works of faith. But in the days following Israel's salvation, He will begin His summation. And He will recap it all. Imagine those coming days. Everything that the Lord has been emphasizing from the beginning will hit the Earth in an explosive and concise restatement.

He will probably not leave much out, but will instead touch all of His previous major points and do so in such a way that the world will not be able to ignore Him. Did He confront nations with His power and glory in biblical times? He will do so again. Did He manifest himself in amazing demonstrations of fire from Heaven? He will do so again.

In fact, the Lord will trumpet forth the clearest and most comprehensive sound ever heard by one generation concerning the realities of Heaven and Earth. His final work on Earth will so harmonize His people with the truth of the heavenly realms that many who are lost among the nations will see and be compelled to attend His feast. Then, finally, God will see His house filled up and He will rejoice.

PART THREE

God's Hidden Road

"Jesus said to him, 'I am the way.'"

John 14:6

CHAPTER 15

A BARRAGE OF STORIES

Heaven's Agenda

In the light of God's great promises, how are we to respond? Since we are anticipating a season in which God will sum up before the nations His ongoing eternal work among men, what is to be our present priority? Of course, the answer is that we must draw close to Him and seek to recognize and understand His sovereign initiatives in our own generation.

What good does it do to speak of God's activities at the end of this age, if we do not perceive His present work? And of course, we do want Him to arise in fresh ways today. But do we even realize what we are asking for? For example, Isaiah prophesied that the Lord would ride into Egypt on a swift cloud (Isaiah 19). But what would happen when He did so? Many Egyptians would turn against each other causing great national division. Then the economy would turn sour causing many people to become deeply troubled. Finally, the Lord would give to Egypt foolish leadership so that the nation's problems would be compounded (See vs. 1-15). Does any of this sound familiar?

In our day, many believers have been praying over a number of years that the Lord would arise powerfully in our land. But many have also become discouraged because they expected immediate glorious times with many people being born of the Spirit and many experiencing physical healing. Of course, all of us want to see such a great national spiritual awakening. But the parallels between what Egypt experienced many years ago with what is presently occurring among us are quite amazing. Is it that the Lord heard our prayers and began to arise in our nation in ways few were expecting?

Today, like in ancient Egypt, division runs deep in America. Many are in a rage at those on the opposite side of the political spectrum. Meanwhile, our economy has been badly shaken and our political leadership seems to not understand their great need for humility before God.

So what is happening? God's relentless agenda is emerging out of Heaven. When Jesus instructed us to pray for God's Kingdom to come, He was telling us to invite Heaven's program. And while He has heard our invitation, His response has not been exactly what we expected. But it is the one that Heaven has deemed appropriate. Ultimately, only one agenda will survive human history, and it won't be ours, and it most certainly won't be the Islamists, secular humanists, Communists, or the Capitalists. God is arising for the sake of His own name. God's Kingdom is emerging.

Heaven's Storyline

Similarly, when Jesus ministered in Israel two thousand years ago, He wasn't exactly what people were expecting. Instead of a glorious king, He came as one casting seed into various kinds of ground, declaring that the results would be very mixed. Some people's hearts were as good fertile ground, while others were as stony or thorny ground. But the seed sown into all the various hearts was the same; it was the gospel of the Kingdom of

God. So how is it that such a pure Source and such a powerful message would have such mixed results? Could the condition of the individual people's hearts make that much of a difference?

Often He would deliver His Word and then conclude with a prophetic declaration that went something like this: "Let hearing occur in those who want to hear." [9] Then one day after Jesus had told the parable of the sower, some listeners along with the twelve came to Him and asked its meaning (Mark 4:10). Upon seeing their hearts to understand, He told them that the mystery of God's Kingdom was now given to them.

Why would the Lord open up the mysteries of eternity to these particular people and not to others who had also heard the same parable? Was it that their hearts were good ground? And what was it that revealed their better heart condition? Very simply, they came to Him and asked for insight. For the rest, Jesus said that all things would come in parables.

I used to think that He was referring only to how He would speak to the crowds—that His teaching would be in the form of parables. But that is not exactly what He said. He actually said that all things (i.e., *everything*) in life would come to them in parables.

A parable is simply an illustrative story. And in our day, everybody is confronted from every direction by the various storylines of those with something to sell. The Capitalists have a storyline. The Socialists have a storyline. The promoters of Darwin's theories have theirs as well. And on it goes. For those who do not know God, all of life is a barrage of stories. But for those who turn to God and ask questions, He offers insights into the mysteries of His Kingdom, truth that will set men free.

In Jesus' day it was no different. The Pharisees, the Sadducees, the Zealots, the Romans etc., all had their various

---

9   I'm rephrasing Jesus' well-known words: "He who has ears to hear, let him hear." But I'm emphasizing the prophetic power of His command to let hearing occur. Whatever was hindering the ability to hear would now be rendered inoperative in those who wanted to understand. They would now be able to perceive God's message and Messenger.

agendas and promotional stories. When Jesus showed up with His parables, to many people He was just another voice among many with an agenda to promote. So they did not even bother to come to Him and ask for insight.

But He was not just another voice among many. He was the Lord God of Heaven and Earth. And He was announcing the only agenda that had a future, one that would endure beyond the boundaries of time itself.

Obscuring The Truth

One unique aspect of Jesus' stories is that they had a two-fold function—they obscured the truth from some people and illustrated the same truth to others. As a result, a great separation began to occur; Jesus came to cause division (Matthew 10:34-36). In fact, He stated that the reason He spoke to the nation in parables was so that in hearing His message, they would not understand lest they should turn and have their sins forgiven (Mark 4:11, 12).

Essentially, His teaching was as a sword that made a separation in the Jewish nation, assuring destruction to many and salvation to others. Many in Israel were choosing a wide road to great loss and others were discovering the narrow road to life. Keep in mind that as many would reap devastation, God's strategy was that they would come to their senses, cry to Him for mercy, and be saved. In other words, though destruction begins in this life because of the hardness of the human heart, such ruin does not have to be mankind's eternal destiny. God's intent is that mercy would triumph over judgment. As a result, many Jews who rejected Christ in His earthly ministry, later realized their great loss, repented, and then received Him in the power of the Holy Spirit causing the Jewish Church to grow by many thousands in the first century.

God's truth always divides; it separates soul from spirit, and judges the motives of men's hearts. As a result, people divide from each other because some will hear and respond to His Word while others will not. For them more destruction lies yet in their future.

So here is a question: Was Christ's intention to obscure the Kingdom from the very people to whom He was sent to reveal it? The answer is—absolutely, if further judgment was what they needed to awaken them.

Thousands of years after God rode into Egypt on a cloud, that nation today continues very divided, its leadership has not turned to the Lord, and its economy remains weak. Yet Isaiah informs us that massive spiritual revival will one day come to Egypt (Isaiah 19:18-25). The only question to consider is how long it will take before the hearts of the Egyptian people become fertile ground for the Word of the Kingdom. How much further pain lies in their future? And who is God sending to sow seed in their midst in our day?

But we need to face the same question as we consider not only our nation, but also the Christian Church here. Can we say that the hearts of God's people in America are all as good fertile soil for the Word of the Kingdom?

And if not, can it be that the Holy Spirit who has been poured out to reveal Christ as Lord, is presently withholding insight from us because there is so much stony and thorny ground in our midst? And also, how much pain lies in our future until we turn to God with a whole heart?

Revealing The Truth

Jesus then asked His disciples a rather obvious question: Would people buy a lamp in order to stick it under a bushel? Of course not. Yet that is exactly what God was doing. Jesus would proclaim truth, obscure it in a story, and then release hearing in those who had come to the end of their personal road of destruction.[10]

---

10   The pain in their lives due to their sinful choices had in fact turned out to be God's plow preparing them to receive the seed of His Word.

111

But God was not hiding truth because He wanted to keep the listeners at a distance—it was just the opposite—He wanted Israel to draw near. This truth is confirmed throughout the Law and the Prophets. Again and again, the Lord called His people to come to Him; how often He wanted to gather them together as a hen gathers her chicks, but many simply would not come.

Today it is the same. The whole Earth is coming to a great confrontation with the living God. He is going to sum up what He has been saying for thousands of years. It is crucial that in our generation we turn from our ways and listen for what our part is to be in preparation for those coming days.

Notice Jesus' next words:

> For there is nothing hidden which will not be revealed, nor has anything been kept secret but that it should come to light. If anyone has ears to hear, let him hear. (Mark 4:22, 23)

How He wanted people to hear. How He wanted them to see the foolishness of their ways, and turn to Him and be saved. In fact, He even said that as listeners we could determine the quantity of our hearing. The measure we would use would determine what He would measure back to us (Mark 4:24).

To illustrate this, let us suppose that someone offered to give one hundred dollar bills to all who came to him. All we would have to do is bring whatever container we wanted filled. If someone brought a small drinking glass, he would indeed walk away with more than he had before. But how wise would be the one who brought a dump truck?

God has hidden His Kingdom so that we might turn from our destructions and cry out to Him not halfheartedly but with a wide-open heart. To this generation, I believe the Lord would say, "Let hearing come to those who have ears to hear."

CHAPTER 16

CHRIST, THE DOOR OF ACCESS

Wading Through The Stories

It is crucial that we hear the Lord's Word to each of us as we peer into the years immediately ahead. God's Kingdom is emerging on the Earth, and yet many of His people while regularly attending Church meetings, face a barrage of stories in His house as well as in the world.

From one preacher, we hear about a coming pre-tribulation Rapture; from another, we hear the storyline about the Church going through the Great Tribulation. But too often, what has been called prophetic has been in reality simply the teaching of a particular system of eschatological thought (i.e., teaching pertaining to the subject of the last days). But we need more; we need to hear from God.

It is not that the Lord cannot speak through such presentations. Obviously, He can. But how much of what we are hearing is the speaker's interpretation of various Bible verses based on a certain systematic approach to the Scriptures? To be clear, we do not need more believers educated in the finer points

113

of the various schools of *end time* thought. While this can be helpful to some degree, we must become trained in loving God and discerning His voice in the midst of all the stories.

There is a way forward. It will not be found when the various schools of thought with wrong conclusions repent and join the correct one. Rather, it will occur as God brings together His people around the person of Christ and we learn to love each other in spite of our differences. Normal Christianity is revealed when the Lord puts together brethren of different persuasions and then teaches them how to hear His voice through each other.

Such a scenario only occurs when we acknowledge that the Holy Spirit has been poured out in order to guide us into the truth (John 16:13). In other words, we are all on a journey, and we are called to take it together.

Journeying Together

To be clear, there is nothing wrong with studying theology. In fact, the Lord specifically calls some to such disciplines. But when we gather with God's people and share from the Scriptures, we must present Christ, not mere theological information. Rather than Calvinism, Calvinists must preach Christ from their Calvinist perspective. Rather than Arminianism, Arminians must proclaim the Lord Jesus to God's people rather than simply an Arminian theological position. And we must use wisdom when we bring an emphasis that we know differs from brethren with whom we are in fellowship. If we do not trust the Holy Spirit to fulfill His ministry of guiding us into the truth together, we will take that job to ourselves, speak aggressively, and bring division to God's house.

One difficulty we face is that we are not all on the same timetable; we must be patient with each other. How wise am I if I expect others to immediately agree with my interpretation of a certain Scripture verse if the Lord took five years of "fine-tuning" to bring me to that view? And on the other hand, what if my conclusions are off and it is not them but me who yet needs the greater adjustment?

But when all is said and done, some will simply not hear the Lord's Word because of the condition of their hearts. To them, the Word of the Lord will seem as only one more story among all the rest found within the Christian world.

The problem is not that God does not know what He wants to say, or that He does not know how to speak clearly. Just like in Israel, to whatever degree His Word in the Church is obscured, it is because of the condition of our hearts.

And then, along with this particular problem, what is to be done when those who teach and preach do not hear Him clearly? The content of their ministry has become in some measure simply another story among many instead of clear words from the Lord. Here is one of the significant problems facing the Church today: too many in Christian leadership are promoting something other than, or something along with the Lord's Word, the Lord's agenda.

As a result, the many ministries and local churches of a region are unable to express one heart and one mind concerning our identity. We may all move as one concerning a particular project, for example an evangelistic crusade, a regional ministry to feed the poor, etc. But as far as being a distinct unique people, moving together with one voice, we simply fall short.

But God's Church shall ultimately come to one mind and speak with one voice to the nations. Jesus committed himself to this end when He promised to so effectively build together His people that the gates of hell would fail in its assaults.

The question facing us is whether we believe His claims or not. How authentic is our faith if we settle for a unity only of those in our particular theological camp? And how is it even possible to get from where we are to Christ's stated goal?

Thieves

We must set our hearts upon the person of the Lord Jesus as the author as well as the focus of our faith. It is not that someday He will build God's house; He is doing so right now before our eyes. And as He works, He is speaking to us; we must listen carefully. He has made the distinct promise that we can discern His voice (John 10).

At the same time we need to heed a clear warning. Jesus stated to some religious leaders that one purpose He had in coming was not only to give sight to the blind but to cause blindness in those who could see (John 9:39-41). These Pharisees, convinced that they could see spiritually quite well apart from Him, closed the door to God's solution for their sinful condition. Thus, thinking they saw, they became established in their blindness. On the other hand, those who confessed their inability to see accurately in the spiritual realms apart from Christ gained access through God's door into His sheepfold—those without sight had their eyes opened.

Our entrance today into God's sheepfold remains the same; we enter through the person of the Lord Jesus (John 10:7). But notice something with me. We do not enter only once, but gain access regularly to His people to both give and receive from them (John 10:9). We must do so through Him, not through some other means. For example, when leaders use their academic training rather than the Lord's present emphasis as the basis for speaking, they gain access amiss. When teachers teach because they hold a position in the Church rather than because the Lord has given them something to say, they have stepped onto "the platform" through the wrong door. When a musician leads out in a song because he or she is the "worship leader," rather than because Jesus wants to sing that song in the midst of the congregation (Hebrews 2:12), he or she has stepped out into the midst of the sheepfold actually drawing attention away from Him, the One we are supposed to be worshiping!

All of us have failed on this issue of proper access many times. And Jesus said that those who function in this manner are thieves (John 10:1). In other words, we literally steal the glory and attention due to the Lord Jesus and allow it in some measure to come to us. But whenever it dawns on any of us what we have done, our first response must be to repent, step out of the way, and then help everyone to refocus on Him.

However, if we refuse to repent and rather persist in our ways, we will begin to slowly move toward the same heart condition exhibited by the Pharisees. Thinking we see, we will gradually lose our sight and settle for a form of religion marked by a slow decrease of God's power in our midst. This process has been repeated consistently throughout Church history.

But brethren, I am confident of better things concerning you, yes even the fruit that accompanies salvation. God is preparing His Church for glorious days ahead. May He continue to woo us to himself. May He continue to draw our attention away from ourselves and upon His glorious majesty. He is the door of access to His people. If we would participate accurately in His work as He builds His glorious house among us, we must listen carefully for His voice and move out according to His Word and His timing.

CHAPTER 17

THE WAY FORWARD FROM HERE

A Coming Awakening

As God's people look toward the coming years, we simply cannot keep *doing church* as we have up to this point. Change is on the horizon. It is just not appropriate to say that we can see really quite well in the realm of the Spirit, thank you very much. Rather, we must cry out to the Lord Jesus to open the eyes of our hearts. If Paul prayed that God would open the Ephesian believers' spiritual eyes so that they could more intimately experience the hope that comes from His call (Ephesians 1:18), then should we not also seek to be filled with an informed hope as we peer into the time ahead? Lord, open our eyes that we might see what was in your heart when you called us.

The American Church needs to be awakened—not just to the many needs around us, but to the Lord and to the priorities of His heart. Paul tells us that we have already been blessed with every spiritual blessing in the heavenly realms in Christ (Ephesians 1:3). He does not tell us that we must somehow attain to them; we simply need our eyes opened to see what is already ours.

For example, when you first hear the sound of your alarm clock from the midst of a deep sleep, it is awakening you to see your bedroom. It is not as though the furniture suddenly appears from nowhere. The dresser, the lamp, the closet, and so on, were all present even though you were totally unaware of them. All the clock did was awaken you to what was already there.

Similarly, a great awakening is coming to the American Church. The Lord intends to open the eyes of His people to what He has already purchased for us. It is ours not because of our works or worth, but because in His great mercy and grace, He paid the necessary price. Everything needed to build His glorious house and to fulfill our destiny as His people is now made available to us in His Son—the grace to heal the sick, raise the dead, receive words of wisdom, bear the presence of God into our surroundings, etc.

God's Road

The price has been fully paid. No one can possibly conceive of any higher price tag. To think that God himself came to the Earth to bear and wash away our sins—how amazing! But what was He purchasing at such a cost? Should we think only in terms of Heaven and spending eternity with Him? Or are there yet vast consequences to be realized on Earth before the final days of history are wrapped up? And if so, how do we get there from where we are today?

There can be only one answer. We must discover and then learn God's road. He has poured out His Spirit in order to open the eyes of our hearts to see His path set before each of us. When Jesus stated in John 14:6 that He was the way (Greek–HODOS, a road), He was telling us that He himself is God's road. All through the Scriptures, God's people have cried out to learn His ways, His road.

Then when He came to the Earth and grew into manhood, He brought the ways of God into crystal clarity for all to see. And while we can learn them by reading the gospel accounts of His life, death, and resurrection, there is more. He promised not to leave us as orphans; He would come to us in the power of the Holy Spirit. In fact, He said that He would send His Spirit to *us* in order to convict *the world* (John 16:7, 8). He wanted to cause a growing conviction of sin, righteousness, and judgment to come upon the nations by pouring His Spirit upon His people.

Unbelievers would discover in their hearts a growing sense of guilt about their sins because before their very eyes are a people believing in Christ as resurrected and ruling (John 16:9). Then they would find within themselves a growing awareness that righteous living and attitudes are available to the human race because in their neighborhoods are people living not by what they see but by what they cannot see (John 16:10). And finally, there would surface within the lost a foreboding sense of coming judgment because they are aligned with someone diametrically opposed to the One being revealed through the believers.

But if the Holy Spirit has indeed come, then why are the nations not more changed? Is it because we have not yet accurately learned God's road? Is it that too many have thought of Christ only as a door for access into Heaven instead of a road to be learned and traveled throughout their lives?

Living Expectantly

Again, great awakening(s) lies in our future. It will not occur simply that we might see the needs of mankind, but a highway lying before us. God's intent is to reveal His answer for what ails the human race through His people as they travel wisely on His road.

For example, when David saw his nation in trouble, he did not simply rise up as the king to fix what was wrong. He cried out to know God's road, God's ways (Psalm 25:22, 4). David knew that he was a man in desperate need of God's mercy. Not only was the nation in trouble, but he was too unless the Lord was merciful to him.

How foolish it is to think that we can fix what ails our nation; we cannot even fix ourselves! How frustrating it is to be broken people trying to fix a broken Church and a broken society. We are constantly aware of how we fall short of God's glory, and how often we misrepresent Him. And yet, as we wait upon Him and look to Him, He promises to teach us His ways.

Ah, but that is the point. We have to wait upon the Lord. Those who wait are basically saying to Him, "I need you to come and give me wisdom in this situation. I need to know your timing concerning what and when to speak or act." Waiting on the Lord expresses the humble hearts of those who know they cannot fix what is wrong around them. But waiting is not inactivity; it is living expectantly with an ear to hear. And Jesus commanded that such people would indeed be enabled to hear Him.

Tempted To Get Off the Road

We are examining the way forward to the final days of human history. God has set before us His highway, even His Son. The problem is that as we move forward in Him, resistance against us will arise not only from unbelievers, but also from those within Christianity who do not trust Him alone for their righteousness (i.e., trusting in their own success in ministry or in holding a certain ministerial position), or who find their identity in past tasks He has given them rather than in an ongoing intimacy with Him. Sadly, many have been sidetracked from God's road.

As a result, shaking is coming to Christ's Church. Many will rediscover their calling to walk in a close love relationship with Him. But others will see their positions in the Church as turf to defend when God unexpectedly reveals himself through simple and sometimes theologically untrained believers who just want more of Him.

What will be our response when He speaks? And what if His instruction is that we quietly serve others who do not agree with us? Our confidence must be in Him and His unstoppable agenda. God alone knows where He wants to take us and how we will get there. It is only as we live in close communion with Him that we will know His will for our lives. He has given us everything we need for this life in Jesus Christ, the words to speak, actions to take, and the power to resist the temptations that cause us to veer off the road He has set for us.

But the minute we step off that road by reverting to our own thinking, and then begin speaking and acting with critical and unforgiving attitudes, we will lose our way. We will stumble badly even though our reasoning seems logical and our theology correct. Right reasoning and sound doctrine are necessary, but God is after more than right reasoning and sound doctrine; He must have a bride whose heart is only for Him. That means God, our Creator, and our Father must be obeyed, His will must be our will without exception.

And if His agenda is that we sit quietly while others speak, will we obey? What if our place of service in the Church is such that many expect us to speak? If we do so simply because of others' expectations rather than because the Lord has given us words of wisdom and life, how have we in any way furthered His agenda? We will have simply muddied the waters. And are they not muddy enough already?

But as we learn Christ, and keep turning to Him no matter the cost, there shall arise in the coming days and generations a people through whom will increasingly flow a crystal clear river of life.

Here is the hope for the nations. They do not need more religious rules thrown at them; they need Christ. To the degree that we walk in harmony with Him, we will be useful in His plan of bringing redemption to the world. On the other hand, if we consider with pride our theology, our finances, our numbers, our training, and so on, compared with others in God's house, we will have disqualified ourselves from the outset.

Grace in Heaven, Increasing Grace on Earth

The truth is that there is far more pride in our hearts than we are aware of. And God hates pride probably as much or more than any other sin. But the good news is that while He resists those who are proud, He will give grace to the humble (1 Peter 5:5). Here is our way forward. Here is His plan for increasing His grace among us. We must humble ourselves. Today there is no lack of grace in Heaven to heal the sick on Earth. At the same time, there is a distinct lack of such grace in much of Christ's Church. But God intends for such spiritual wealth to increase among His people not only for His sake but also for the sake of countless desperate lost souls who simply have no answers to their physical as well as their spiritual dilemmas.

So let me make a clear promise to you. In coming days the Lord will give each of us opportunities to humble ourselves. When He does so, it will seem too costly at first. But don't buy the lie; rather, embrace your cross. Our first tendency will be to justify ourselves, or to prove someone wrong and ourselves right, or to make sure that we get our *say* in, or to make sure that others notice our involvement in a particularly successful ministry, etc. But let's humble ourselves instead. As we do so, His grace will increase in our lives. While it may be imperceptible at first, it will surely grow; His promise is sure.

To confirm this strategy, consider the Lord's Prayer. I always thought that Jesus' priority concerning God's will was that one day it would be done on Earth as perfectly as it is in Heaven. But that is not exactly what He said. While it is true that in the new heavens and on the new Earth, our obedience will be perfect, there is a present application. At least in Matthew's gospel, His clear reference is to doing His will with no self-promotion. We are to give, pray, and fast in secret (Matthew 6:1-18). In Heaven there is no promotion of self. One angel tried it once, got kicked out, and took some others with him. Clearly, God will not allow such grievous and offensive attitudes in His eternal abode. Yet, these very sins are prevalent in His house on Earth. Therefore, the power and glory that fills Heaven is limited in its expression among us.

Closing Promise

But God has promised that as surely as He is eternal, the glory filling Heaven will also fill the Earth. We cannot produce it; we cannot *speak it into existence.* But we can humble ourselves before Him and before others so that the grace filling Heaven might increase in our lives.

The one perfect example that we have in Scripture is Jesus himself, who, because He was full of grace, revealed God's glory on Earth. (John 1:14)

We have no other option; we must learn of Him, for Jesus is God's way set before us to The Coming Increase of Christ in His House.